30.

Irish
potato
recipes

Irish
potato
recipes

Gill & Macmillan

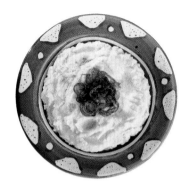

Published in Ireland by
Gill & Macmillan Ltd
Hume Avenue, Park West
Dublin 12
with associated companies throughout the world
www.gillmacmillan.ie
Text © Salamander Books 2002
0 7171 3356 7

Published by arrangement with Salamander Books Ltd, London
Printed in Spain

A CIP catalogue record for this book is available from the British Library.

1 3 5 7 9 8 6 4 2

Designed, edited and produced by Hilton/Sadler

Contents

Introduction

The Irish are renowned throughout the world for the friendliness and hospitality they show to guests, be they friends or strangers. Such has been the case since pagan times, when even kings and princes were governed by the Brehon Laws – precise rules concerning hospitality and etiquette originally formulated in the fifth century.

At this time, wealth was reckoned according to the number of cattle a person owned. Young bulls were slaughtered for veal and meat was salted down for winter use. Sheep were plentiful in the uplands and swine fed on acorns in the oak forests. In addition to domesticated animals, wild boar, deer and huge Irish hares abounded, and the skies were full of game birds.

Archaeological evidence of a tenth-century Viking city on the site of modern-day Dublin proves that in addition to beef, mutton and pork being on the menu the ancient Irish also feasted on seafood, apples, strawberries, cherries, plums, hazelnuts, grapes and figs – though the poor were more likely to have subsisted on gruel and nettle soup.

The potato, often associated with Ireland, was actually unknown in Ireland until it was introduced in Elizabethan times by Sir Walter Raleigh, when he was Mayor of Youghal, County Cork. It soon proved popular, becoming a staple food for the poor. The infamous potato famine of 1845–1849 was an entirely artificial tragedy – Ireland at the time was bursting with food, but the cereals and dairy produce were for export only, and so the peasants died of starvation in their millions when the potato crop failed in a series of disastrous harvests.

The versatile potato

Helped by the different types – floury or waxy – and the number of varieties, potatoes can be boiled, stuffed, roasted, fried, baked, sautéed, casseroled, steamed or mashed. They can be formed into fritters and croquettes; made into scones; used as a cover for pies or to make the bases for tarts and pizzas; incorporated into puddings, biscuits, cakes, breads and pastries; or they can be used as a thickening agent for soups, sauces and casseroles.

With growing consumer interest in the quality of food in general, tastes and demands are changing. Potato growers, who at one time concentrated primarily on yield and disease resistance, are now more concerned with growing potato varieties for their flavour and cooking characteristics. As a result, old varieties are being restored to favour and new ones are being researched and developed. These potatoes may cost a little more, but good food always carries a premium.

Potato varieties

Depending on the variety and when it is harvested during its growing cycle, a potato can weigh anything from less than 25 g (1 oz) to more than 450 g (1 lb). Some are round in shape, others long and pointed, but most are oval- or kidney-shaped. Skin colour ranges from almost transparent in newly formed potatoes through pale golden brown and pink to red, brown or nearly black. Skin texture is also variable – smooth or netted like some melons – and flesh may be white, cream, pink-ish, or various shades of soft yellow. These are all obvious characteristics; what cannot be judged by looking, however, is whether the flesh will be waxy or floury when cooked.

Commercial as well as domestic growers divide potatoes into earlies, second earlies and main crop, depending on when they are harvested. Size is not a reliable guide to when the potato was harvested, as, for example, some main-crop varieties can be small in size.

Early varieties (new potatoes) are usually available from late May through to August and are most flavourful when used fresh. Try to buy these potatoes from a store with a high turnover, and cook and consume them within 48 hours of purchase if possible.

New potatoes are a good source of vitamin C, and they have a more pronounced flavour, thinner skins, and a more waxy texture than main-crop varieties. They are best boiled and larger ones make good French fries. Most will sauté well but they do not mash successfully.

Main-crop varieties are usually available from September onward. The texture depends on type – some being waxy, some floury – although in late autumn potato flesh tends to be waxy, becoming more floury after storage.

Waxy or floury

As a guide, floury types of potato include Cara, Catriona, Golden Wonder, Kerr's Pink, King Edward, Maris Piper, Pentland Crown, Pentland Dell, Pentland Squire and Wilja. These potatoes are suitable for mashing, sautéeing and roasting, but they tend to break up on the outside when boiled.

Waxy types of potato include Arran Comet, Belle de Fontenay, Charlotte, Desirée, Estima, Home Guard, Jersey Royal, Marfona, Maris Bard, Maris Peer, Pentland Javelin, Pink Fir Apple, Romano and Ulster Sceptre. These potatoes have a firm flesh ideal for boiling and make good salad ingredients. They are not as successful when fluffy baked potatoes are wanted or for mashing.

To test whether a potato is waxy or floury, dissolve 1 part salt in 11 parts water. Add the

potato to this brine solution – a waxy variety of potato will float while a floury one will sink.

Tasty tips

• If a soup or casserole is too salty, add some chopped raw potato to the liquid and cook until the potatoes are tender. The potato flesh should absorb some of the excess salt.

• The size of the French fries, or chips, affects the amount of fat they absorb, and so determines how fattening they are – long, thin French fries have a greater surface area than short, plump chips, and so absorb more fat and contain more calories. Likewise, crinkle-cut potatoes have an increased surface area and so contain more calories.

• Use left-over mashed potatoes, or mash other left-over potatoes, to thicken soups, sauces and casseroles.

• Left-over boiled potatoes can be made more appetizing by dicing or slicing them and frying them until they are crisp and golden before sprinkling them with paprika.

• The amount of butter, milk or cream added to mashed potatoes depends on how soft you want the mixture to be.

• For a party effect, spoon mashed potatoes into a piping bag fitted with a large star nozzle. Pipe the mash in swirls on an oiled baking sheet and brown in a moderate oven.

• To make a very quick and easy pastry case, press mashed potatoes into a flan tin or shallow baking dish to line it. Bake at 190–220° C (375–425° F/Gas 5–7) until brown.

• A simple way to make ready-sauced potatoes is to cut them into thickish slices, put into a saucepan and half fill with water. Add a lump of butter or 1–2 tablespoons of olive oil. Cover the pan tightly and boil briskly for 10–15 minutes. Check the water level toward the end of the cooking time and add more if necessary. Tip the potatoes and cooking liquid into a serving dish. If the potatoes are cooked and there is too much liquid, remove them and boil the sauce to thicken and reduce it.

Metric or imperial

It is impossible to convert metric into imperial with complete accuracy – by necessity, figures are often rounded up or down to the nearest convenient figure. In view of this, in the recipes in this book you should follow only the metric or the imperial quantities within the same recipe – do not mix and match them.

When teaspoon or tablespoon measures are given, simply use approximate quantities. Dry ingredients should be measured as flat spoonfuls, unless otherwise stated. With liquid measures, 1 tablespoon is equivalent to 15 ml and 1 teaspoon is 5 ml.

Soups and starters

The number of recipes for potato soups is vast – they can be simple or a complex blend of ingredients, smooth or chunky, homely or haute cuisine. First courses range from corn and potato chowder to crunchy potato skins with yogurt, avocado and bacon.

Potato, tomato and basil soup

- 675 g (1½ lb) new potatoes, coarsely chopped
- 55 g (2 oz) butter, chopped
- 1 large onion, finely chopped
- 1 fresh bay leaf
- 5 sprigs fresh thyme
- 1.5 litres (3 pints) vegetable stock or water
- 4 tablespoons olive oil
- 450 g (1 lb) well-flavoured tomatoes, peeled, seeded and chopped
- Leaves from small bunch fresh basil
- Red wine vinegar
- Salt and pepper

Melt the butter gently with the onion, bay leaf and thyme in a little of the stock or water. Add the remaining stock or water, the potatoes and salt to taste. Bring to the boil, then simmer until the potatoes are falling apart. Discard the herbs and pass the potatoes through a vegetable mill or purée very briefly, then press through a sieve. Return to the pan.

Meanwhile, cook the tomatoes in 1 tablespoon of the oil until lightly thickened. Beat to a nubbly purée, then add to the soup and reheat. Purée the basil with the remaining oil, seasoning and a little red wine vinegar.

Serve the soup in warm bowls with a spoonful of the basil mixture floating on top and black pepper ground over the surface.

Serves 4

Watercress soup

- 600 ml (1¼ pint) chicken, veal or vegetable stock
- 225 g (8 oz) old potatoes, peeled and chopped
- 1 onion, chopped
- 25 g (1 oz) butter
- 2 bunches watercress, chopped
- About 300 ml (10 fl oz) creamy milk
- Freshly grated nutmeg
- Salt and pepper
- Chopped fresh chives, to garnish

Cook the onion gently in the butter until it is softened but not coloured. Then stir in the potatoes, add the stock and simmer until the potatoes are just tender.

Add the watercress and simmer for 30 seconds. Pass the soup through a vegetable mill or purée very briefly in a blender (otherwise it will become "gluey") and then press the soup through a sieve.

Return the soup to the rinsed pan and add enough of the milk to give the required consistency. Add the nutmeg and seasoning, then heat to just below simmering point; don't let the soup boil. Serve garnished with chives.

Serves 4

Opposite above: Potato, tomato and basil soup
Opposite below: Watercress soup

Leek and potato soup

- 750 g (1½ lb) potatoes, diced
- Knob of butter
- 1 tablespoon olive oil
- 500 g (1 lb) leeks, sliced
- 1 tablespoon plain flour
- 500 ml (16 fl oz) chicken stock
- Salt and pepper
- 1 bay leaf
- 2 sprigs tarragon or 1 teaspoon dried tarragon
- 500 ml (16 fl oz) milk

Heat the butter and oil in a large saucepan. Reserve a few pieces of leek for garnish, if preferred, and then add the remaining leeks and potatoes, and cook, stirring, for about 5 minutes, or until the leeks are slightly softened. Stir in the flour, and then pour in the stock, stirring all the time.

Transfer the leek and potato mixture to a clay pot that has been soaked in cold, fresh water for 15 minutes. Stir in the seasoning, bay leaf and tarragon. Cover the pot and place it in a cold oven. Set the oven at 200° C (400° F/Gas 6). Cook for 50 minutes. Gradually stir the milk into the soup. Cook, covered, for a further 40 minutes, or until the vegetables are tender. Serve the soup chunky or blended smooth in a liquidizer. Taste for seasoning before serving, garnished with the reserved leek.

Serves 4

Potato and coriander soup

- 900 g (2 lb) potatoes, peeled and diced
- Small bunch fresh coriander
- 2 onions, chopped
- 2 garlic cloves, chopped
- 2 tablespoons olive oil
- 1.2 litres (2 pints) chicken or vegetable stock or water
- Salt and pepper

Cut the coriander leaves from the stems. Chop the leaves and reserve. Tie the stems together. Fry the onion and garlic gently in the oil until softened but not coloured. Stir in the potatoes and coriander stems, cover and cook over a low heat for 5 minutes. Pour in the stock or water and seasoning. Bring to the boil, then simmer until the potatoes are falling apart.

Discard the coriander stems. Pass the potatoes through a vegetable mill, or purée very briefly in a blender, and then press through a sieve. Return the soup to the pan, add the coriander leaves and reheat gently. Do not allow the soup to boil.

Serves 4

Above: Potato and coriander soup

Left: Leek and potato soup

Crunchy potato skins

- 6 medium-sized floury potatoes
- 4 tablespoons cooking oil
- 6 rashers smoked streaky bacon
- 2 small avocado pears
- 1 garlic clove, crushed
- 2–3 teaspoons lemon juice
- 2–3 teaspoons natural yogurt
- 2 drops Tabasco sauce
- Salt and pepper
- Fresh herb sprigs, to garnish

Preheat the oven to 200° C (400° F/Gas 6). Scrub potatoes and prick them all over with a fork. Bake in the oven for 1 hour, or until just tender. Remove them from the oven and turn the heat up to 220° C (428° F/Gas 7).

Pour the oil into a shallow roasting dish and put into the oven to heat. Remove the rind from the bacon and grill the rashers until they are crisp and golden. Drain well.

Peel and stone the avocados and mash the flesh with garlic, lemon juice, yogurt, Tabasco and salt and pepper. Cut the potatoes in half lengthways. Using a teaspoon, scoop out most of the potato flesh, leaving a layer next to the skin. Reserve the potato for making potato waffles (see p. 32). Sprinkle the skins with salt and place in the hot oil. Baste with oil, then turn them hollow side up and bake in the oven for 25 minutes, basting regularly, or until the potatoes are golden and crunchy.

Drain the potatoes on absorbent kitchen towel, then fill the cavities with the avocado cream. Cut the bacon into small strips and scatter over the potatoes. Garnish with herbs and serve at once.

Serves 4–6

Potato soup

- 900 g (2 lb) potatoes, sliced
- 60 g (2 oz) butter
- 2 onions, sliced
- 1 small carrot, sliced
- Bouquet garni
- Salt and freshly ground black pepper
- 1 litre (2 pints) chicken or vegetable stock
- 550 ml (1 pint) milk
- Freshly chopped chives

Melt the butter in a large pan, add the prepared vegetables and cook slowly until they are soft, but not browned. Stir in the seasonings and stock and bring to the boil. Cover and simmer slowly for 30 minutes, or until the vegetables are tender.

Press the soup through a sieve or blend it in a liquidizer or food processor until smooth. Return the soup to the pan and add the milk, then heat the mixture gently until it is almost boiling. Season to taste and serve garnished with a few freshly chopped chives.

Serves 8

Crunchy potato skins

Spinach and potato croquettes

- 675 g (1½ lb) potatoes, boiled in their skins, then peeled
- 550 g (1¼ lb) fresh young spinach *or* 225 g (8 oz) cooked spinach
- 1 egg yolk
- 2 tablespoons grated mature Cheddar cheese
- Freshly grated nutmeg
- About 3 tablespoons seasoned flour
- 2 eggs beaten
- About 85 g (3 oz) fine cornmeal (polenta) or dry breadcrumbs
- Salt and pepper
- Oil for deep frying
SAUCE
- 550 g (1¼ lb) well-flavoured, fleshy tomatoes, peeled, seeded and chopped
- 5 spring onions, finely chopped
- Salt and pepper

To make the sauce, mix all the ingredients together, season, and then cover and chill in the refrigerator.

Wash the fresh spinach and cook in just the water clinging to the leaves, stirring occasionally, until wilted and all the surplus moisture has evaporated. Chop the spinach and squeeze out as much water as possible. If using frozen spinach, allow it to thaw, then squeeze out the moisture. Pass the potatoes through a vegetable mill or sieve. Beat in the spinach, egg yolk and cheese, then season with nutmeg, salt and pepper. Form into balls or small sausage shapes, and roll in the seasoned flour to coat them lightly and evenly. Dip in the egg, then coat in fine cornmeal or breadcrumbs. Half fill a deep frying pan with oil and heat to 180° C (350° F). Add the croquettes in batches and fry until brown and crisp. Transfer to paper towels with a slotted spoon and drain. Serve hot with the sauce.
Serves 4–6

Mozzarella fritters

- 550 g (1¼ lb) potatoes, freshly boiled in their skins
- 2 egg yolks
- 40 g (1½ oz) butter, melted
- 150 g (5 oz) mozzarella cheese, cut into fingers
- 2 eggs, beaten
- 100 g (3½ oz) dry breadcrumbs
- Salt and pepper
- Oil for deep frying

Peel the cooked potatoes and return them to the heat briefly to dry out before mashing. Remove from the heat, beat in the egg yolks, butter and pepper to make a stiffish dough.

When the dough is cool enough to handle, put some in the palm of your floured hand and place a finger of mozzarella in the middle. Seal the potato over the cheese and roll into a sausage shape. Coat it in beaten egg and then roll it in breadcrumbs to coat it evenly. Repeat with the remaining potato and cheese. Half fill a deep frying pan with oil and heat to 190° C (375° F). Fry the fritters in batches until they are crisp and golden. Transfer to paper towels with a slotted spoon and drain. Serve hot.
Serves 4

Opposite above: Spinach and potato croquettes
Opposite below: Mozzarella fritters

Corn and potato chowder

- 6 medium-sized potatoes, peeled
- Chicken or vegetable stock
- 1 onion, finely chopped
- 30 g (1 oz) butter or margarine
- 1 tablespoon flour
- 110 g (4 oz) cooked ham, chopped
- 4 fresh cobs of corn or 110 g (4 oz) canned or frozen corn
- 700 ml (1½ pint) milk
- Salt and dash Tabasco sauce
- Parsley, finely chopped

Quarter the potatoes and place them in a deep saucepan. Add stock to cover and the onion, then bring the mixture to the boil. Lower the heat and simmer, partially covered, for about 15–20 minutes, or until the potatoes are soft. Drain the potatoes, reserving 300 ml (10 fl oz) of the cooking liquid. Mash the potatoes and combine them with the reserved liquid.

Melt the butter or margarine in a clean pan, add the ham and cook briefly. Stir in the flour and pour over the potato mixture, mixing well.

If using fresh corn, remove the husks and silk and, holding one end of the corn, stand the cob upright. Use a large, sharp knife and cut against the cob vertically from top to bottom, just scraping off the kernels. Add the corn and milk to the potato mixture and bring almost to the boil. Do not boil the corn rapidly as this will toughen it. Add a pinch of salt and a dash of Tabasco, and garnish with parsley before serving.

❧ When cooking corn on its own, add the salt just before serving. Cooking corn with salt toughens it.

Serves 4–6

Potato soup with salmon and chives

- 6 medium potatoes, peeled and chopped
- 170 g (6 oz) salmon, cutlet or tail piece
- 2 tablespoons finely chopped fresh chives
- 55 g (2 oz) butter
- 1 onion, finely chopped
- 2 leeks, chopped
- 1 bay leaf
- 575 ml (1 pint) chicken or fish stock
- 575 ml (1 pint) milk
- Salt and freshly ground black pepper

Place the salmon in a small saucepan, just barely cover it with water, and poach gently for about 10 minutes, or until the fish is cooked. Remove from the water, skin, remove the bones and flake the flesh. Add the cooking water to the stock.

Melt the butter in a large saucepan and cook the onion and leeks until tender but not coloured. Add the potatoes, bay leaf, seasoning and the stock, and cook until the potatoes are soft. Purée the mixture in a food processor, first removing the bay leaf. Return to the saucepan.

Now add the chives, milk and salmon and gently bring to the boil. Adjust the seasoning to taste and serve hot.

Serves 6

Opposite: Corn and potato chowder

Salads

Waxy potatoes, especially new ones, often make the best salads, and the peak time for making salads is when the best potatoes are available. For the maximum flavour absorption, toss the potatoes in any dressing as soon as they are cooked.

Potato salad with herb sauce

- 675 g (1½ lb) potatoes, unpeeled
HERB SAUCE
- 2 garlic cloves
- leaves from bunch fresh parsley
- 15 fresh mint leaves
- 10 fresh basil leaves
- 6 anchovy fillets
- 1 tablespoon capers
- 1 tablespoon Dijon mustard
- 150 ml (5 fl oz) virgin olive oil
- Salt and pepper

To make the herb sauce, crush the garlic with a pinch of salt in a pestle and mortar, then work in the herb leaves, followed by the anchovy fillets and capers. Mix in the mustard, then pour in the oil very slowly, mixing the ingredients together well, as when making mayonnaise. Season with pepper and set sauce aside.

Cook the potatoes in boiling water until they are tender. Drain, leave until cool enough to handle but still warm, then dice them and mix with the herb sauce immediately. Leave to cool before serving.

Serves 4

Potato and asparagus salad

- 300 g (10 oz) small new potatoes, unpeeled
- 300 g (10 oz) asparagus
- 4 tablespoons olive oil
- 2 teaspoons lemon juice
- 25 g (1 oz) Parmesan cheese, cut into very thin slivers
- Finely chopped parsley, to garnish
- Salt and pepper

Trim the asparagus, discarding the woody ends of the stalks. Cut into 2.5 cm (1 in) lengths, keeping the tips and stalks separate.

Add the stalks to a pan of boiling salted water and cook for 5 minutes. Then add the asparagus tips and cook for a further 3–4 minutes, or until they are just tender. Drain, reserving the water. Spread the asparagus stalks and tips on a pad of paper towels, and cover.

Boil the potatoes in the reserved cooking water until they are tender.

Meanwhile, whisk together the oil, lemon juice and seasoning. Drain the potatoes and toss them with the dressing, cheese and asparagus. Sprinkle over the parsley and serve warm.

Serves 4

Opposite above: Potato salad with herb sauce
Opposite below: Potato and asparagus salad

Warm potato and mushroom salad

- 450 g (1 lb) potatoes
- 375 g (12 oz) mixed mushrooms
- Olive oil for greasing
- Leaves from a bunch of parsley or basil
- 4 garlic cloves, crushed
- Salt and freshly ground black pepper
- Flat-leaf parsley sprigs and basil leaves, to garnish

Thinly slice the mushrooms and potatoes. Preheat the oven to 180° C (350° F/Gas 4). Generously oil an ovenproof dish that will hold the potatoes and mushrooms in a layer no more than 4 cm (1½ in) deep. In a large bowl, toss together the mushrooms, potatoes, parsley or basil, garlic and salt and pepper.

Spread the potato mixture into the dish in an even layer and bake for about 45 minutes, or until the potatoes are tender, turning the mixture halfway through. Leave it to stand for a couple of minutes. Garnish with flat-leaf parsley and basil and serve.
Serves 4

Potatoes vinaigrette

- 450 g (1 lb) potatoes, sliced
- 1 tablespoon finely chopped coriander
- 1 tablespoon olive oil
- 2 tablespoons malt vinegar
- Salt and pepper
- 2 green onions, coarsely chopped
- 8 ripe olives, pitted and halved

Steam the potatoes over boiling salted water for 7–10 minutes, or until they are tender. Place in a serving bowl and add the coriander.

In a jar with a tight-fitting lid, shake together the oil, vinegar, salt and pepper. Pour the dressing over the potatoes and toss to combine. Sprinkle the onions and olives over salad.
Serves 4–6

Above: Potatoes vinaigrette
Left: Warm potato and mushroom salad

Potato salad with fennel

- 450 g (1 lb) new potatoes
- 115 g (4 oz) French beans, trimmed
- 115 g (4 oz) trimmed fennel
- 25 g (1 oz) stoned olives
- 2 tablespoons capers, drained
- 2 tablespoons chopped fresh chives
- 2 teaspoons chopped fresh tarragon
- 3–4 tablespoons virgin olive oil
- Juice ½ lemon
- 2 eggs
- 400 g (14 oz) can artichoke hearts, drained and halved

Cook the potatoes in a pan of lightly salted boiling water for 10–12 minutes, or until just tender. Drain and place in a large bowl. Blanch the beans in boiling water for 1–2 minutes, or until just tender, drain and refresh under cold water; pat dry. Slice the fennel very thinly and halve the olives. Add to the potatoes with the beans, capers and herbs. Stir in the oil and lemon juice and set aside until the potatoes are cold.

Hard boil the eggs, plunge in cold water and peel. Roughly chop and add to the salad with the artichoke hearts. Toss well and serve at once.

Serves 4–6

Warm new potato, celery, Stilton and walnut salad

- 450 g (1 lb) new potatoes, unpeeled, halved if large
- 2 garlic cloves
- 115 g (4 oz) walnuts, coarsely chopped
- 4 tablespoons walnut oil
- 115 g (4 oz) Stilton cheese, crumbled
- 1 celery heart, sliced
- Fresh thyme leaves, to garnish
- Salt and pepper

Cook the potatoes in boiling salted water for 15–20 minutes, or until tender. Meanwhile, put the garlic, a pinch of salt, half the walnuts and the walnut oil in a blender and mix to a thick sauce.

Drain the potatoes thoroughly. Immediately tip them into a warm serving bowl and add the walnut sauce, cheese, celery and remaining nuts. Toss lightly and sprinkle with a few thyme leaves and serve at once.

Serves 4

Above: Warm new potato, celery, Stilton and walnut salad

Left: Potato salad with fennel

Hot potato salad with bacon

- 6–8 even-sized waxy potatoes
- Pinch salt
- 115 g (4 oz) bacon
- 1 onion
- 120 ml (4 fl oz) white wine vinegar
- 120 ml (4 fl oz) water or beef stock
- 3 tablespoons sour cream (optional)
- 2 tablespoons chopped parsley
- Salt and pepper

Boil the potatoes in their jackets in lightly salted water to cover. When the potatoes are just tender, drain and peel while still hot. Cut into thin slices and place in a serving dish.

Fry the bacon in a large frying pan or sauté pan. While the bacon is frying, chop the onion very finely. Once the bacon is a pale golden brown add the onions and continue to sauté slowly, until they become transparent but not brown. Remove the pan from the heat and carefully pour in the vinegar and the water or stock. Do this gradually so that the hot fat does not spatter.

Bring the liquid to the boil and remove it from the heat. Stir in the sour cream, if using, and pour the mixture evenly over the potatoes. Lift the potatoes so that the dressing runs all over and beneath them. Sprinkle with salt and pepper and parsley. Serve immediately.

Serves 6–8

Potato and chick-pea salad

- 450 g (1 lb) small new potatoes
- 2 tablespoons olive oil
- 1 onion, sliced
- 2 garlic cloves, sliced
- 1 teaspoon cumin seeds
- 450 g (1 lb) plum tomatoes, peeled
- 400 g (14 oz) can chick-peas, drained
- Salt and freshly ground black pepper
- 2 tablespoons fresh mint, roughly chopped

Either scrub or peel the potatoes, according to preference. Cut them in half unless they are very small. Boil the potatoes in salted water for 10 minutes, or until they are soft, and then drain.

Meanwhile, heat the oil in a large saucepan. Add the onion and cook for 10 minutes, or until soft and golden brown. Add the garlic and cumin seeds and cook for 3–4 minutes. Cut the tomatoes into eighths and add them to the pan. Cook for a few minutes until the tomatoes just begin to soften.

Add the drained chick-peas and the potatoes. Cook for a few minutes until warmed through. Season with salt and pepper and stir in the mint. Serve hot or cold.

Serves 4–6

Opposite: Hot potato salad with bacon

Right: Potato and chick-pea salad

Jacket potato salad

- 450 g (1 lb) small old potatoes, unpeeled
- 175 ml (6 fl oz) natural yogurt
- 2–3 tablespoons lemon juice
- 5 spring onions, finely chopped
- 2–3 teaspoons Dijon mustard
- 1 red pepper, sliced
- Salt and pepper

Thread the potatoes on skewers and bake in a preheated oven at 200° C (400° F/Gas 6) for about 35 minutes, or until tender.

Meanwhile, stir together the yogurt, lemon juice, spring onions, mustard and seasoning.

Cut the potatoes into quarters while still warm, mix with the red pepper and toss with the dressing. Serve at room temperature.

Serves 4

Potato, smoked trout and dill salad

- 675 g (1½ lb) new potatoes, unpeeled
- 4 tablespoons mayonnaise
- 4 tablespoons natural yogurt
- 1 teaspoon lemon juice
- 4 teaspoons wholegrain mustard
- 4 tablespoons chopped fresh dill
- About 175 g (6 oz) skinned smoked trout, flaked
- Salt and pepper

Boil the potatoes for 10–15 minutes, or until they are tender. Meanwhile, mix together the mayonnaise, yogurt, lemon juice, mustard, dill and the seasoning.

Drain the potatoes and leave them to cool for 5 minutes. Toss them with the smoked trout, and then mix with the dressing. Serve warm or leave until cold, then cover and chill.

Serves 4

Classic potato salad

- 675 g (1½ lb) new or waxy potatoes, unpeeled
- 4 sprigs fresh mint
- 2 tablespoons wine vinegar
- 1 teaspoon Dijon mustard
- 5 tablespoons flavourless vegetable oil
- 1 teaspoon olive oil
- Small bunch spring onions finely chopped or chives, chopped
- Salt and pepper

Boil the potatoes with the mint until they are tender. Then drain and cut into halves or quarters, depending on their size.
Meanwhile, whisk together the vinegar, mustard, oils and seasoning.

Toss the potatoes while they are still warm with the dressing and spring onions or chives. Leave them to cool before serving.

Serves 4–6

Opposite above: Jacket potato salad
Opposite middle: Classic potato salad
Opposite below: Potato, smoked trout and dill salad

Snacks and light meals

Busy cooks are always looking out for new ideas for snacks and light meals. Potatoes are an invaluable ally for all those times when you want to prepare quick, nutritious and tempting food without spending too much time in the kitchen.

Traditional potato scones with herbs

- 450 g (1 lb) floury potatoes, boiled in their skins
- 20 g (¾ oz) butter
- 1–1½ tablespoons chopped, mixed fresh herbs – such as parsley, thyme, marjoram, rosemary, tarragon and basil
- 4 spring onions, finely chopped
- 25 g (1 oz) Parmesan cheese, freshly grated (optional)
- About 115 g (4 oz) plain flour
- Salt and pepper

Pass the cooked potatoes through a vegetable mill, potato ricer or sieve, and then stir in the butter, herbs, spring onions, cheese (if using) and seasoning. Turn the mixture out on to a lightly floured surface and leave it to cool.

Work in the flour; you will need about a third of the volume of the potato for this. Roll out to about 8 mm (⅓ in) thick. Dust lightly with flour and cut into triangles or squares as preferred. Re-roll the trimmings as necessary.

Cook the scones on a dry, non-stick griddle or in a dry, non-stick frying pan over a low to moderate heat for about 3 minutes on each side. Serve warm as part of a cooked breakfast, or served with cheese, cold meat and salads, or simply buttered. The scones can be kept for 1–2 days in an airtight container if necessary.

Serves 4

Irish potato cakes

- 450 g (1 lb) mashed potatoes
- 55 g (2 oz) rindless bacon
- 20 g (¾ oz) butter
- Large handful fresh parsley, finely chopped
- Plain flour
- Bacon fat, oil or butter for frying
- Salt and pepper

Grill the bacon until it is crisp, then drain on paper towels and crumble. Next, mix the butter, parsley and seasoning into the potatoes, and stir in the bacon pieces. Form the mixture into flat cakes and dust lightly in flour.

Fry the cakes in a little hot bacon fat, oil or butter until they are crisp and brown on both sides.

Serves 4

Opposite above: Traditional potato scones with herbs

Opposite below: Irish potato cakes

Potato and broccoli gratin with goat's cheese

- 675 g (1½ lb) potatoes, unpeeled
- 300 g (10 oz) broccoli florets
- 15 g (½ oz) butter
- 4 tablespoons double cream or fromage frais
- 1 x 85 g (3 oz) log of goat's cheese, thinly sliced
- Freshly grated nutmeg
- Salt and pepper

Boil the potatoes until they are very tender and drain. Peel when they are cool enough to handle. Meanwhile, boil the broccoli until it is tender. Drain thoroughly, then purée in a food processor or blender.

Mash the potato with the butter and cream or fromage frais, then mix in the broccoli. Season with salt, pepper and nutmeg. Spoon the mixture into a buttered baking dish, level the surface and cover with the slices of goat's cheese. Place under a preheated grill until the cheese is beginning to bubble and brown.

Serves 4

Barbecued potato and egg peppers

- 250 g (8 oz) potatoes, cooked
- 4 small green peppers (capsicums)
- 4 hard-boiled eggs, shelled
- 3 tablespoons mayonnaise
- 2 teaspoons French mustard
- 4 teaspoons chopped fresh chives
- 1 teaspoon paprika
- ½ teaspoon garlic salt
- Pepper
- Parsley sprigs, to garnish

Cut away a thin slice from the stalk end of each pepper and remove the core, seeds and pith. Coarsely chop the hard-boiled eggs and potato. Then add the mayonnaise, French mustard, chives, paprika, garlic salt and pepper to taste, and mix the ingredients together well.

Carefully spoon the mixture into the green peppers. Wrap each one separately in lightly buttered, double thickness foil and barbecue on a rack, or directly in medium-hot coals, for about 30 minutes, or until the peppers are tender. Turn them over occasionally during the cooking. Serve garnished with sprigs of parsley.

Serves 4

Above: Barbecued potato and egg peppers

Left: Potato and broccoli gratin with goat's cheese

Potato pizza with tomatoes, aubergines and basil

- 675 g (1½ lb) floury potatoes, freshly boiled in their skins
- 25 g (1 oz) butter
- 1 egg, beaten
- 1 tablespoon finely chopped fresh rosemary
- 40 g (1½ oz) Parmesan or mature Cheddar cheese, freshly grated
- Olive oil for brushing and trickling
- 350 g (12 oz) well-flavoured tomatoes, sliced
- 1 small aubergine, about 175 g (6 oz), thinly sliced
- 115 g (4 oz) fontina or feta cheese
- About 8 black olives, preferably oil-cured
- About 8 basil leaves, coarsely shredded
- Salt and pepper

Peel the boiled potatoes and pass them through a vegetable mill, potato ricer or sieve. Mix in the butter, egg, rosemary, cheese and seasoning. Press into a lightly floured 25 cm (10 in) pizza pan. Brush lightly with olive oil and arrange the tomato slices over the top, taking them right to the edge. Then add the aubergine slices, tucking them between the tomato slices. Grate or crumble over the fontina or feta cheese, sprinkle with pepper, dot with the olives and trickle over a little olive oil. Bake near the top of a preheated 220° C (425° F/ Gas 7) oven for 25–30 minutes. Sprinkle with basil and serve.

Serves 2

Irish fish cakes

- 700 g (1½ lb) cooked potato, mashed
- 700 g (1½ lb) cooked fish, flaked (use white fish, salmon or trout; oily fish is less successful in fish cakes)
- 25 g (1 oz) butter
- 1–2 tablespoons freshly chopped mixed herbs, including fennel and tarragon
- Salt and freshly ground black pepper
- 3 medium eggs, beaten
- Flour
- 120 g (4½ oz) fresh breadcrumbs
- Oil for shallow frying

Remove all skin and bones from the flaked fish, then mix in a bowl with the potato, butter and seasoning. Bind the mixture together with as much egg as required, then, with floured hands, shape it into four large or eight medium fish cakes.

Dip the cakes in the remaining egg, then coat them in breadcrumbs. Repeat the procedure, using an extra egg if necessary, and shallow fry the fish cakes in hot oil until they are golden brown, turning once. Serve hot.

Serves 4

Potato pizza with tomatoes, aubergines and basil

Cheesy potato and fennel layer

- 675 g (1½ lb) potatoes, unpeeled
- 450 g (1 lb) small fennel bulbs
- 2 eggs, beaten
- 225 g (8 oz) ricotta cheese
- 5 spring onions, chopped
- 85 g (3 oz) Gruyère cheese, finely grated
- 2 tablespoons breadcrumbs
- Salt and pepper

Boil the potatoes until they are cooked but still firm. Drain and, when they are cool enough to handle, peel and thinly slice them.

Meanwhile, trim the fennel, reserving the feathery green fronds. Slice the fennel bulbs and boil in salted water for 10 minutes. Drain well.

Beat the eggs, seasoning and reserved fennel fronds into the ricotta cheese. Layer one-third of the potatoes in a buttered baking dish. Cover with half the fennel, spread with half the ricotta mixture and sprinkle over one-third of the spring onions and Gruyère. Repeat the layers, then cover with the remaining potato. Mix the remaining spring onions and Gruyère with the breadcrumbs, sprinkle over the potato and bake in a preheated oven at 200° C (400° F/Gas 6) for 30 minutes, or until golden.

Serves 4

Buttery onion squares

- 450 g (1 lb) potatoes, unpeeled, freshly boiled
- 1 small onion
- 175 g (6 oz) butter
- 350 g (12 oz) self-raising flour
- 2 teaspoons baking powder
- About 120 ml (4 fl oz) buttermilk or milk mixed with natural yogurt
- Milk for glazing
- Finely grated cheese for sprinkling
- Salt and pepper

Peel the boiled potatoes when they can be handled and pass them through a vegetable mill, potato ricer or sieve. Leave them to cool.

Meanwhile, fry the onion gently in 20 g (¾ oz) of the butter until they are softened but not coloured. Leave it to cool.

Sift the flour, baking powder and some salt into a bowl. Rub in the remaining butter, then lightly mix in the potatoes, onion and buttermilk to make a smooth, soft dough. Turn the dough on to a lightly floured surface and knead it lightly, and roll out or pat it into 2 cm (¾ in) thickness.

Using a sharp knife, cut the dough into 5 cm (2 in) squares and place them about 5 cm (2 in) apart on a buttered baking sheet. Brush the tops with milk and sprinkle lightly with cheese. Bake in a preheated oven at 220° C (425° F/Gas 7) for 12–15 minutes, or until well risen and lightly browned.

Makes about 15

Opposite above: Cheesy potato and fennel layer

Opposite below: Buttery onion squares

Potato waffles

- 185 g (6 oz) mashed potato
- 2 tablespoons hot milk
- 6 teaspoons plain flour
- 30 g (1 oz) butter, melted
- Celery salt and pepper
- 2 eggs, beaten
- 45 g (1½ oz) butter
- 6 spring onions, chopped
- 375 g (12 oz) mixed mushrooms
- 315 ml (10 fl oz) thick sour cream
- 1 tablespoon chopped fresh parsley
- Chopped chives and parsley sprigs, to garnish

In a bowl, beat the potato, milk, flour and melted butter together until smooth, then season with celery salt and pepper. Add the eggs and mix the ingredients thoroughly together.

Heat an electric waffle iron and brush it with oil. Fill one half with potato batter, clamp down the lid and cook for 2–3 minutes, or until the steam stops escaping and the waffle is golden and crisp. Remove it from the iron and keep it warm. Repeat until all the batter is used up.

Melt the butter in a saucepan and fry the spring onions and mushrooms until they are slightly softened, then add the cream and bring to the boil, stirring continuously until thick. Stir in the parsley.

Serve the waffles topped with the creamed mushrooms and garnished with chopped chives and sprigs of parsley.

Serves 4

Hash browns with relish

- 750 g (1½ lb) potatoes
- 6 rashers smoked streaky bacon
- Salt and pepper
- 45 g (1½ oz) butter
- 2 tablespoons vegetable oil
- 1 onion, finely chopped
- 220 g (7 oz) can chopped tomatoes
- 2 teaspoons tomato purée (paste)
- ½ teaspoon sugar
- 1 teaspoon horseradish sauce
- 1 teaspoon French mustard
- ½ teaspoon chopped fresh thyme

Cook the potatoes in a large saucepan of boiling salted water for 10 minutes. Drain and cool under cold running water, then pat dry.

Remove the rind from the bacon and chop the bacon into very small cubes. Coarsely grate the potatoes and mix them together with the bacon. Season with salt and pepper.

Melt the butter and 1 tablespoon of the oil in a large frying pan and cook spoonfuls of the potato mixture over a moderate heat until they are crisp and golden. Turn them over and cook the other sides and then remove them from the pan. Drain on absorbent kitchen paper and keep them warm while preparing the remaining hash browns.

Heat the remaining tablespoon of oil in a pan and gently fry the onion until slightly softened. Add the tomatoes, tomato purée (paste), sugar and salt and pepper and cook until thick and pulpy. Stir in the horseradish, mustard and thyme and cook for a further minute. Serve the hash browns with spoonfuls of the tomato relish.

Serves 4

Rosti

- 750 g (1½ lb) potatoes, scrubbed
- 1 small onion
- 4 rashers smoked streaky bacon
- 60 g (2 oz) Austrian smoked cheese
- Salt and pepper
- 45 g (1½ oz) butter
- Basil sprigs, to garnish

Place the potatoes into a saucepan of salted water, bring to the boil and simmer for 5 minutes. Remove the pan from the heat, drain and allow the potatoes to get cold.

Coarsely grate the potatoes and onion into a large bowl. Remove the rind from the bacon and cut the bacon into very thin strips. Cut the cheese into small chunks and, using 2 forks, toss the bacon and cheese into the potato mixture and season with salt and pepper.

Melt the butter in a large frying pan, add the grated mixture and cook over a moderate heat for 10–15 minutes. Then press well together, turn over and cook the other side for a further 5 minutes. Turn out on to a warmed plate, cut into wedges and serve at once, garnished with sprigs of basil.

Serves 4

Top: Potato waffles
Above: Hash browns with relish
Left: Rosti

Potato cakes and mango sauce

- 225 g (8 oz) potatoes, peeled
- 115 g (4 oz) butternut squash, peeled
- 15 g (½ oz) butter, diced
- 1 egg yolk
- 45 g (1½ oz) Cheddar cheese, grated
- 1 tablespoon grated onion
- 2 teaspoons chopped fresh coriander
- A little flour seasoned with salt and pepper
- 1 egg, beaten
- 115 g (4 oz) Brazil nuts, ground
- 115 g (4 oz) mango, peeled and chopped
- 1 spring onion, trimmed and chopped
- 1 small garlic clove, crushed
- ½ small, fresh, green chilli, seeded and chopped
- Juice of 1 lime
- Vegetable oil for deep frying

Cube the potatoes and the squash and cook them until they are tender. Drain, mash well and stir in the butter, egg yolk and cheese until it has melted. Stir in the onion and coriander and season. Leave until cold. Shape the mixture into 8 small rounds and flatten them into thin patties. Dust with seasoned flour, dip in the egg and then the ground nuts to coat the cakes on all sides.

Place all the remaining ingredients, except the oil, in a blender or food processor and purée until fairly smooth. Stir in a little water if the sauce is too thick. Heat about 1 cm (½ in) vegetable oil in a non-stick frying pan and fry the potato cakes, in batches, for 2–3 minutes on each side, or until golden. Change the oil and repeat, if necessary. Drain well on absorbent kitchen paper and serve hot with the mango sauce.

Serves 8

Vegetarian hash potatoes

- 575 g (1¼ lb) potatoes, peeled
- 45 g (1½ oz) butter
- 1 onion, thinly sliced
- 1 teaspoon chopped fresh sage
- 1 teaspoon chopped fresh rosemary
- 3 tablespoons natural yogurt
- 45 g (1½ oz) Cheddar cheese, grated
- 1 teaspoon wholegrain mustard
- 1 teaspoon Worcestershire sauce

Cut the potatoes into chunks, place them in a pan, cover with cold water and bring to the boil. Cook for 15–20 minutes, or until they are tender. Drain and roughly mash.

Melt 15 g (½ oz) of the butter in a large, non-stick frying pan and fry the onion and herbs for 10 minutes, or until the onion is soft and golden. Then combine the remaining ingredients.

Add the mashed potatoes to the frying pan and stir in the yogurt mixture, flattening the mixture out to the sides of the pan. Cook over a high heat for 5–6 minutes, or until golden underneath. Using a spatula, turn the hash, a little at a time, and brown the other side. Serve straight from pan.

Serves 4

Potato cakes and mango sauce

Potato and onion flan

- 200 g (7 oz) plain flour
- Pinch of salt
- 100 g (3½ oz) unsalted butter, diced
- 1 egg yolk
- 2 tablespoons iced water

FILLING

- 450 g (1 lb) waxy potatoes
- 25 g (1 oz) butter
- 2 large onions, thinly sliced
- 1 teaspoon chopped fresh rosemary
- ½ teaspoon caraway seeds
- 200 ml (7 fl oz) low-fat fromage frais
- 25 g (1 oz) vegetarian Cheddar cheese, grated
- Freshly grated nutmeg

Preheat the oven to 200° C (400° F/Gas 6). Sift the flour and salt into a large bowl and rub in the butter until the mixture resembles fine breadcrumbs. Make a well in the centre and work in the egg yolk and water to form a soft dough. Knead on a floured surface, wrap and chill for 30 minutes. Roll out thinly and use the dough to line a deep 23 cm (9 in) fluted flan tin. Prick the base, then chill for 20 minutes. Line with foil and baking beans and bake blind for 10 minutes. Remove beans and foil and bake for a further 10–12 minutes, or until crisp.

Increase the oven temperature to 230° C (450° F/ Gas 8). Cook the potatoes for 15 minutes, or until just tender. Allow them to cool and then peel and cut them into very thin slices. Melt the butter and fry the onions, rosemary and caraway seeds for 10 minutes, or until golden. Spread the onion mixture over the pastry case and arrange the potato slices over the top. Beat the remaining ingredients together, spread over the potatoes and bake at the top of the oven for 15 minutes, or until golden.

Serves 6–8

Above: Potato and onion flan

Left: Vegetarian hash potatoes

Jacket potato fillings

The jacket potato is everybody's favourite, be it for a light snack, an accompaniment to another dish or as a substantial meal in itself. This is not surprising, as there can be few more versatile, inexpensive and absolutely delicious vegetables than the potato.

Cooking the perfect jacket potato

Before you start to choose a filling, you need to know how to cook the perfect potato. Choose potatoes of even size – about 275 g (10 oz) each is about right – to keep cooking time consistent.

To cook the potatoes, preheat your oven to 200° C (400° F/Gas 6). Scrub unwashed potatoes thoroughly and prick them all over with a fork. This will prevent the potato from bursting during cooking. If you wish, you can brush the potatoes with a little melted butter or sunflower oil. Then place them on a baking tray and bake for 1–1¼ hours, or until they are soft when gently squeezed. Serve them lightly seasoned with a knob of butter or with the filling of your choice.

You do not need any special equipment to bake potatoes, but you can reduce cooking time by about 10 to15 minutes by pushing a metal skewer through the middle of each one or using a potato roaster – a device with four metal spikes to accommodate four potatoes. Both these methods allow the heat to be conducted to the middle of the potato, so decreasing cooking time.

Using a microwave dramatically reduces cooking time, but unfortunately you miss out on the lovely crispy skin produced in a conventional oven. Scrub and prick the potatoes, but do not brush them with oil or butter. Arrange them in the microwave in a circle on a piece of kitchen towel. Cook on full power, turning them halfway through. One potato takes 4–6 minutes; two 10–12 minutes; and four 18–20 minutes in a 650W microwave oven.

Ratatouille

- 4 large baking potatoes
- 2 tablespoons olive oil
- 1 Spanish onion, sliced
- 1 garlic clove, crushed
- ½ small aubergine, chopped
- ½ red pepper, seeded and chopped
- ½ green pepper, seeded and chopped
- 400 g (14 oz) can chopped tomatoes
- 1 tablespoon tomato purée
- 1 teaspoon chopped fresh oregano
- Few fresh basil leaves, torn into pieces
- 5 tablespoons red wine or vegetable stock
- Salt and pepper

Cook the potatoes as directed (see left). Heat the oil in a large frying pan and sauté the onion until it starts to soften. Add the garlic and cook for 1 minute. Then stir in the aubergine and peppers and fry over a medium heat until it just begins to soften.

Add the tomatoes, tomato purée, oregano, basil and wine or stock. Bring gently to the boil, then reduce the heat and simmer for 30 minutes, or until the liquid has slightly reduced.

When the potatoes are cooked, cut them in half and place them on a serving plate. Season the ratatouille to taste and spoon the mixture over the potatoes. Serve immediately.

Serves 4

Opposite: Ratatouille

Smoked cod and broccoli filling

- 4 large baking potatoes
- 225 g (8 oz) smoked cod, skinned
- 140 ml (5 fl oz) milk
- Salt and pepper
- Pinch of grated nutmeg
- 120 g (4 oz) broccoli florets
- 30 g (1 oz) butter
- 30 g (1 oz) plain flour
- Oil

Bake the potatoes as directed (see p. 36). Put the cod in an ovenproof dish. Pour over the milk and season with salt, pepper and nutmeg. Cover with foil and cook alongside the potatoes for 20 minutes. When the fish is cooked, drain off the liquid and make it up to 280 ml (10 fl oz) with water, then set aside. Flake the fish and set aside.

Cook the broccoli florets in lightly salted boiling water for 5 minutes. Drain well and set aside. Melt the butter in a saucepan. Stir in the flour and cook over a low heat for 1 minute. Remove from the heat and gradually add the reserved cooking liquid, stirring well after each addition. Return the pan to the heat and cook gently until it has thickened, stirring constantly.

Stir in the fish and broccoli. Cut the cooked potatoes in half and scoop out the flesh. Mash well and spoon into a piping bag. Spoon the fish mixture into half of the potato skins and pipe the potato on top. Discard the remaining potato skins. Brush with a little oil and return to the oven for about 15 minutes to brown the tops. Or brown them under a preheated grill and serve at once.
❥ This dish is not suitable for microwaving.
Serves 4

Salmon with creamy dill sauce

- 4 large baking potatoes
- 30 g (1 oz) butter
- 340 g (12 oz) salmon fillet
- 4 tablespoons dry white wine
- 1 tablespoon chopped fresh dill
- 6 tablespoons crème fraîche
- Fresh dill and lemon twists, to garnish

Cook the potatoes as directed (see p. 36). Melt the butter in a frying pan and cook the fish for 3–4 minutes on each side. Remove from the pan and flake the fish, discarding skin and bones. Add the wine to the pan and bring to the boil. Boil for 1 minute. Stir in the dill and crème fraîche and boil for 2–3 minutes, or until slightly thickened. Add the fish and heat through.

When the potatoes are cooked, cut a cross in the top of each one. Using a clean tea-towel, gently squeeze each potato to open out the cross slightly. Spoon the salmon on top and serve garnished with sprigs of dill and lemon twists.
Serves 4

Above: Salmon with creamy dill sauce
Opposite: Smoked cod and broccoli filling

Easy chilli filling

- 4 large baking potatoes
- 1 tablespoon sunflower oil
- 1 small onion, chopped
- 340 g (12 oz) lean minced beef
- 1 teaspoon chilli powder
- 140 ml (5 fl oz) beef stock
- 200 g (7 oz) can red kidney beans, drained and rinsed
- 4 tomatoes, skinned if preferred, and roughly chopped
- 1 tablespoon tomato purée

Cook the potatoes as directed (see p. 36). Heat the oil in a saucepan and fry the onion until it is just soft. Add the minced beef and continue to cook until browned. Stir in the chilli powder and cook for 1 minute.

Stir the stock, beans, tomatoes and tomato purée into the pan and bring to a gentle boil. Reduce the heat and simmer for 20 minutes, or until the meat is tender. When the potatoes are cooked, cut the top off each one and mash the flesh if preferred. Pour the chilli over the top and serve.

Serves 4

Easy chilli filling

Creamy bacon and mushroom topping

- 4 large baking potatoes
- 6 rashers back bacon
- 60 g (2 oz) butter
- 2 garlic cloves, crushed
- 6 spring onions, sliced
- 225 g (8 oz) mushrooms, sliced
- 1 teaspoon cornflour
- A little milk
- Pinch of grated nutmeg
- 200 g (7 oz) tub fromage frais (8% fat)
- Salt and pepper

Cook the potatoes as directed (see p. 36). Remove the rind from the bacon and discard. Cut the bacon into strips. Melt the butter in a frying pan and sauté the bacon and garlic until the bacon begins to brown. Then stir in the spring onions and mushrooms and sauté for 5–6 minutes, or until the mushrooms are soft.

Mix the cornflour to a smooth paste with a little milk, then stir into the pan. Add the nutmeg and stir in the fromage frais. Bring the mixture carefully to simmering point and simmer for 2 minutes, trying not to let it boil. Season to taste with salt, pepper and nutmeg.

When the potatoes are cooked, cut a cross in the top of each. Using a clean tea-towel, gently squeeze each potato to open out the cross slightly. Spoon the mushroom mixture on top and serve immediately.

❧ Don't use the very low-fat fromage frais in this recipe as it will curdle.

Serves 4

BLT jackets

- 2 large baking potatoes
- 1 tablespoon olive oil
- 4 spring onions, sliced
- 1 garlic clove, crushed
- 200 g (7 oz) can tomatoes
- 1 teaspoon mixed herbs
- 2 rashers back bacon or 4 rashers streaky bacon
- A few crisp lettuce leaves
- 2 tablespoons mayonnaise (optional)

Cook the potatoes as directed (see p. 36). Heat the oil in a small saucepan and sauté the spring onions and garlic for 1 minute, or until just beginning to soften. Stir in the tomatoes and herbs. Bring to the boil, then reduce the heat and simmer gently for 5 minutes, breaking up the tomatoes with the back of a spoon as they cook. Cook the bacon in the oven alongside the potatoes for 15 minutes or under a preheated grill until crisp and golden.

When the potatoes are cooked, cut them in half and, if preferred, mash the flesh. Arrange a few lettuce leaves on top of the potatoes and spoon on the tomato sauce. Top with the bacon and mayonnaise if liked. Serve immediately.
Serves 2

Ham and broccoli stuffed potatoes

- 4 large baking potatoes
- 225 g (8 oz) broccoli florets
- 30 g (1 oz) butter
- 30 g (1 oz) plain flour
- 280 ml (10 fl oz) milk
- Salt and pepper
- Pinch of grated nutmeg
- 60 g (2 oz) sweetcorn kernels
- 175 g (6 oz) ham, diced

Cook the potatoes as directed (see p. 36). Cook the broccoli in lightly salted boiling water for 5 minutes, taking care not to overcook it. Drain well. Melt the butter in a saucepan and stir in the flour and cook over a low heat for 1 minute. Remove from the heat and gradually add the milk, stirring well after each addition. Return the pan to the heat and cook over a low heat until thickened, stirring constantly. Season to taste with salt, pepper and nutmeg. Add the cooked broccoli, the sweetcorn and ham, and heat through.

When the potatoes are cooked, cut them in half and scoop out the flesh. Mash well. Add the broccoli and ham mixture and beat together until well combined. Spoon the mixture back into the potato skins and serve.
Serves 4

Above: BLT jackets
Right: Ham and broccoli stuffed potatoes

Vegetarian main dishes

The cause of vegetarianism has been done untold good by the rich variety of non-meat produce – fruit, vegetables and pulses, in particular – now available all year round, as well as the many exciting and innovative recipes to turn them into mouth-watering main meals.

Creamy potato and vegetable pie

- 450 g (1 lb) floury potatoes, chopped
- 450 g (1 lb) leeks, sliced
- 1 onion, chopped
- 2 tablespoons olive oil
- 175 g (6 oz) mushrooms, sliced
- 1 red pepper, sliced
- 115 g (4 oz) fresh spinach
- 425 g (15 oz) can red kidney beans, drained and rinsed
- 150 g (5 oz) full-fat soft cheese with herbs and garlic
- 2 x 340 g (12 oz) packets puff pastry, well chilled
- Beaten egg for glazing
- Salt and pepper

Cook the potatoes in salted water until tender. Drain and leave until cold. Cook the leeks and onion in oil until softened but not coloured. Add the mushrooms and pepper, and cook until the mushrooms are soft. Stir in the spinach briefly, until it wilts. Remove from the heat and stir in the beans, potatoes and cheese. Leave until cold.

On a lightly floured surface, roll out one piece of pastry to a 33 x 25 cm (13 x 10 in) shape. Place it on a baking sheet. Cover with the potato filling, leaving a 2.5 cm (1 in) border. Roll out the remaining pastry to a slightly larger rectangle and place on top. Dampen the edges of the pastry and seal together. Mark diamonds on the top with the point of a knife. Brush with beaten egg and chill for 20 minutes. Bake in a preheated 200° C (400° F/ Gas 6) oven for 35 minutes, or until well risen and golden.

Serves 6

Potato and bean casserole with tomatoes

- 450 g (1 lb) new potatoes, or old potatoes, cut into chunks
- 225 g (8 oz) haricot beans, soaked overnight and drained
- 1 large onion, chopped
- 2 leeks sliced
- 3 tablespoons oil
- 2 garlic cloves chopped
- 1 teaspoon cumin seeds, crushed
- 1 teaspoon paprika
- 225 g (8 oz) can chopped tomatoes
- 2 tablespoons tomato purée
- 1 litre (1¾ pints) vegetable stock
- 2 tablespoons chopped fresh coriander
- Natural yogurt to serve

Boil the beans with sufficient water to cover for 10 minutes. Meanwhile, heat the oil in a heavy, flameproof casserole and cook the potatoes, onion, and leeks for about 10 minutes, or until the potatoes are pale gold in colour. Stir in the garlic, cumin and paprika and cook for about 1 minute. Then add the tomatoes, tomato purée and stock and bring to the boil. Drain the beans and add to the casserole. Cover and simmer gently for about 1½ hours, or until the beans are tender. Finally, stir in the coriander and seasoning and serve with the natural yogurt.

Serves 4

Opposite above: Potato and bean casserole with tomatoes

Opposite below: Creamy potato and vegetable pie

Potato casserole with yogurt topping

- 700g (1½ lb) waxy potatoes, unpeeled and sliced
- 2 onions, thinly sliced
- 2 tablespoons olive oil
- 3 garlic cloves, finely chopped
- 2 courgettes, sliced
- 2 red peppers, seeded and chopped
- 300 ml (10 fl oz) sieved puréed tomatoes
- Bouquet garni
- 300 ml (10 fl oz) vegetable stock
- 1 tablespoon chopped fresh basil
- 1 teaspoon cornflour
- 300 g (10 oz) thick natural yogurt
- 100 g (3½ oz) mozzarella cheese, grated
- 55 g (2 oz) mature Cheddar cheese, grated
- 55 g (2 oz) breadcrumbs

Heat the oil in a heavy frying pan and cook the onions until they have softened. Add the garlic, potatoes, courgettes and peppers. Cook, stirring, for 5 minutes, then add the puréed tomatoes, bouquet garni, stock and seasoning. Bring to the boil, then cover tightly and simmer for 1 hour, stirring occasionally. Stir in the basil and divide the mixture between four shallow, heatproof dishes.

Blend the cornflour into the yogurt, then mix in half of the cheeses. Season with pepper and spread over the middle of the potato mixture. Mix together the remaining cheeses and the breadcrumbs, and scatter over the yogurt. Place the dishes in a preheated 200° C (400° F/Gas 6) oven, or under a moderate grill for 5–10 minutes, until browned.

Serves 4

46

Top: Curried vegetable burgers
Middle: Potato casserole with yogurt topping
Left: Potato and herb terrine

Potato and herb terrine

- 750 g (1¾ lb) waxy potatoes, unpeeled, thinly sliced
- Handful young spinach leaves
- 2 eggs, lightly beaten
- 350 g (12 oz) crème fraîche
- Leaves from smallish handful mixed fresh herbs, such as parsley and chives, with chervil, tarragon, thyme and sorrel
- 55 g (2 oz) Gruyère cheese, grated
- Pinch cayenne pepper
- Salt and pepper

Place a generously buttered loaf tin in a roasting tin. Add the spinach to a saucepan of boiling water, return to the boil and cook for 1 minute. Drain the spinach, rinse under cold running water, then drain and dry well. Chop finely.

Mix the eggs into the crème fraîche, then add the spinach, herbs, half the cheese, the cayenne pepper and seasoning. Spread a little of the herb mixture over the base of the loaf tin, cover with a layer of potato slices and sprinkle with some of the remaining cheese. Repeat the layering until all the ingredients have been used, ending with the cheese. Cover the tin with foil and pour boiling water around. Bake in a preheated 180° C (350° F/ Gas 4) oven for about 1¼ hours, removing the foil 15–20 minutes before the end of the cooking time. Turn off the oven but do not remove the loaf tin for 15 minutes.

To serve hot, invert the tin on to a warm serving plate. To serve cold, leave the terrine in the tin for 2–8 hours, then run a knife point around the edge to loosen the terrine.

Serves 4

Curried vegetable burgers

- 450 g (1 lb) potatoes
- 1 egg yolk
- 1 onion, chopped
- 2 tablespoons oil, plus extra for frying
- 1 garlic clove, crushed
- 2 slim leeks, finely chopped
- 1 celery stick, finely chopped
- 2 carrots, finely chopped
- 2 teaspoons curry powder
- 2 tablespoons chopped fresh parsley
- Milk (optional)
- Fresh breadcrumbs for coating
- Salt and pepper

Boil the potatoes in salted water until tender. Drain and, when cool enough to handle, peel and mash them with the egg yolk.

Meanwhile, cook the onion gently in the oil until it has softened. Add the garlic, leeks, celery and carrots and continue to cook, stirring occasionally, until the vegetables are tender. Stir in the curry powder for 1 minute.

Mix the curried vegetables and the parsley into the potatoes. Add a little milk if the mixture seems dry. Add seasoning and form into 6–8 flattish cakes. Coat the cakes in breadcrumbs, then fry them in oil for about 3 minutes on each side, or until golden.

Serves 3–4

Traditional vegetable bake

- 3 medium potatoes, cooked and cut into 6 mm (¼ in) slices
- ½ cup black beans, soaked overnight and cooked until tender
- 1 medium cauliflower, divided into florets
- 750 ml (1½ pints) water
- 1 bay leaf
- 300 ml (10 fl oz) milk
- 2 tablespoons sunflower oil
- 1 medium onion, very finely chopped
- 3 tablespoons fine whole-wheat flour
- 1 tablespoon wholegrain mustard
- 1 tablespoon fresh parsley, chopped
- Salt and pepper
- 2 tablespoons butter or margarine

Wash and drain the cauliflower florets. Bring the water to the boil in a large pan, add the bay leaf and a little salt. Plunge the cauliflower into the water, return to the boil, cover and cook for 8–10 minutes, or until the florets are just cooked. Drain, discard the bay leaf and reserve the cooking water. Mix the milk with enough cooking water to make about 475 ml (1 pint).

Heat the oil in a small pan and gently sauté the onion until it is soft. Stir in the flour and cook over a gentle heat for 1–2 minutes. Gradually add the milk and water, stirring all the time to avoid lumps. Add the mustard and cook gently for another 3 minutes. Drain the cooked beans and return them to a large pan, add the cauliflower and mix well. Pour the mustard sauce over the beans and cauliflower and stir in the chopped parsley and seasoning.

Place the mixture in a greased casserole dish. Top with the sliced potatoes, overlapping them slightly, and dot with the butter or margarine. Bake at 180° C (350° F/Gas 4) for 20–25 minutes, or until the top is nicely browned.

Serves 4

Potato ratatouille

- 550 g (1¼ lb) waxy potatoes, cubed
- Olive oil for cooking
- 1 large onion, chopped
- 2 small or medium aubergines, thinly sliced
- 2 red peppers sliced
- 2–3 plump garlic cloves, crushed
- 6 small courgettes sliced
- 3 medium-large, well-flavoured ripe tomatoes, peeled, seeded and chopped
- Leaves from a few sprigs fresh thyme, marjoram and oregano, chopped
- About 10 fresh basil leaves, chopped

Heat a little oil in a large, heavy pan and fry the onion for a few minutes, then add the aubergines and cook for a further few minutes.

Add a little more oil, the peppers and garlic, and cook the ingredients until the peppers begin to soften. Add the courgettes, cook for a few more minutes, then add the potatoes, tomatoes, herbs (except the basil) and seasoning. Cook gently for 30–40 minutes, stirring occasionally, or until the potatoes are tender. Add the basil and cook for another minute. Serve hot, warm or cold.

Serves 4

Above: Potato ratatouille
Opposite: Traditional vegetable bake

Fish main dishes

Fish and other types of seafood are becoming increasingly popular as main meal choices, but the ingredients can be expensive to buy. However, by combining seafood with potatoes, these dishes become far more affordable.

Special fish pie

- 675 g (1½ lb) potatoes, boiled in their skins and peeled
- 115 g (4 oz) butter
- 450 ml (15 fl oz) milk, plus extra for mashing
- ½ onion, chopped
- 1 bay leaf
- 225 g (8 oz) firm white fish fillet, such as cod, haddock or monkfish
- 225 g (8 oz) salmon fillet
- 1 garlic clove
- 150 ml (5 fl oz) mayonnaise
- 115 g (4 oz) peeled, cooked, fresh prawns
- 25 g (1 oz) plain flour
- 225 g (8 oz) tomatoes, peeled, seeded and chopped
- About 2 tablespoons freshly shredded basil

Mash the potatoes with 25 g (1 oz) of the butter, 4 tablespoons of milk and seasoning. Slowly bring the onion, bay leaf and remaining milk to the boil. Add the fish, cover and simmer gently for about 5 minutes. Crush the garlic with a pinch of salt and mix it into the mayonnaise. Remove and flake the fish. Strain the milk. Melt half the remaining butter and stir it in the flour for about 1½ minutes. Add the milk slowly, then bring to the boil, stirring. Cook for 4 minutes. Off the heat, stir in the prawns, tomatoes, basil, fish, mayonnaise and seasoning. Spoon into a baking dish and cover with potato. Dot with the remaining butter and bake in a preheated 190° C (375° F/Gas 5) oven for about 25 minutes.

Serves 4

Haddock supper

- 450 g (1 lb) potatoes, thinly sliced
- 350 ml (12 fl oz) milk
- 350 ml (12 fl oz) double or whipping cream
- 1 fresh bay leaf
- A little nutmeg (optional)
- 900 g (2 lb) smoked haddock, skinned and bones removed
- Leaves from small bunch fresh parsley, chopped
- Firm, ripe, flavoursome tomatoes, peeled and thickly sliced

Heat the milk and cream with the bay leaf and pepper to simmering point. Add the fish and poach until it is just tender. Remove and flake the haddock; reserve the milk. Make a layer of potatoes in a buttered baking dish, sprinkle with parsley and add about one-third of the fish. Sprinkle again with parsley and top with some tomato slices.

Discard the bay leaf from the milk and cream mixture, then pour some into the dish to cover the tomatoes. Repeat the layering, finishing with potatoes on top. Grate over a little nutmeg, if liked, and bake in an oven preheated to 220° C (425° F/ Gas 7) for about 20 minutes. Then lower the oven temperature to 190° C (375° F/Gas 5) and bake for a further 40 minutes.

Serves 4

Opposite above: Haddock supper
Opposite below: Special fish pie

Potato, smoked salmon and dill galette

- 900 g (2 lb) potatoes, peeled and very thinly sliced
- ½ lemon
- 225 g (8 oz) smoked salmon trimmings
- 100 g (3½ oz) unsalted butter, diced
- 90 ml (3 fl oz) soured cream
- 3 tablespoons chopped fresh dill
- Pepper
- Fresh dill, to garnish
- Lemon wedges, to serve

Squeeze the lemon evenly over the smoked salmon. Rinse the potatoes and dry them well on paper towels. Melt the butter gently in a small saucepan and skim off the white foam from the top. Pour 2 tablespoons of the butter into a 23 cm (9 in) non-stick, ovenproof frying pan; keep the remaining butter warm over a low heat.

Arrange one-third of the potatoes in a neatly overlapping layer in the pan, seasoning only with the pepper. Add half the smoked salmon, sprinkle with pepper and the dill, and pour over half of the cream. Top with another layer of potatoes, brushing them with butter and seasoning with pepper. Add the remaining salmon, dill and cream, then finish with the remaining potatoes. Brush with butter and season with pepper. Pour over any remaining cream.

Cook over a moderate heat for 5 minutes until the underside is brown (lift the edge with a palette knife to check). Press firmly and evenly over the surface, cover with a lid or foil and bake in a preheated 200° C (400° F/Gas 6) oven for 40–45 minutes, or until the potatoes are cooked. Loosen around the edges and underneath, place a large warm plate upside down over the pan and invert the galette on to it. Garnish with dill and serve with the lemon wedges.

Serves 4

Fish chowder

- 450 g (1 lb) potatoes, cut into small chunks
- 55 g (2 oz) butter
- 1 large onion, chopped
- 2 plump garlic cloves, chopped
- 4 celery sticks, chopped
- ½ red pepper diced
- 85 g (3 oz) mushrooms, sliced
- 600 ml (1 pint) each fish stock and milk
- Bouquet garni
- 250 g (9 oz) each smoked and fresh haddock skinned and cut into bite-sized pieces
- 115 g (4 oz) peeled prawns
- Cayenne pepper

Melt the butter in a large saucepan and cook the onion, garlic, celery, pepper and mushrooms until they begin to soften. Stir in the potatoes and cook for 2 minutes. Add a large pinch of cayenne, the stock and bouquet garni, bring to the boil, then cover and simmer for 20 minutes. Add the milk and haddocks to the pan, and simmer gently for a further 8–10 minutes, or until the fish flakes. Add the prawns and heat through.

Serves 4–6

Potato and salmon parcels

- 250 g (9 oz) new potatoes, freshly boiled in their skins
- 5 tablespoons virgin olive oil
- 2 shallots, chopped
- Small bunch chives, chopped
- 4 salmon steaks, skinned, boned and chopped

Dice the potatoes and then mix them with 3 tablespoons of the oil, the shallots and half of the chives. Season with pepper.

Cut four circles of foil about 23 cm (9 in) in diameter and another four slightly larger. Divide the potato mixture between the larger circles and add one-quarter of the salmon to each. Sprinkle over the remaining oil and chives, and grind over black pepper. Cover with the smaller circles, fold the edges together firmly and place them on a baking sheet. Bake in a preheated 190° C (375° F/Gas 5) oven for 8–10 minutes. Serve the unopened parcels at room temperature.

Serves 4

Top: Potato and salmon parcels
Middle: Fish chowder
Left: Potato, smoked salmon and dill galette

Cod, prawn and mushroom gratin

- 675 g (1½ lb) medium new potatoes, unpeeled
- 450 g (1 lb) cod fillet, skinned and cut into 2.5 cm (1 in) pieces
- Bouquet garni
- 350 ml (12 fl oz) creamy milk
- 225 g (8 oz) button mushrooms
- 25 g (1 oz) plain flour
- 25 g (1 oz) butter
- 115 g (4 oz) peeled cooked prawns
- 2 teaspoons Dijon mustard
- About 1 tablespoon chopped fresh tarragon or dill
- 85 g (3 oz) Gruyère cheese, grated
- Salt and pepper

Boil the potatoes until they are tender. Drain and thickly slice. Meanwhile, poach the cod with the bouquet garni in the seasoned milk for 5 minutes. Add the mushrooms and cook for an additional 5 minutes. Drain, reserving the milk. Put the fish and mushrooms in a shallow baking dish. Scatter over the prawns.

Heat the reserved milk, the flour and butter, whisking until thickened. Bring to the boil, then simmer for 4 minutes. Discard the bouquet garni and whisk in the mustard, herbs and seasoning. Pour into the dish and stir together gently, leaving the surface level. Cover with overlapping slices of potato, sprinkle over the cheese and place under a preheated grill until just golden.

Serves 4

Classic fish pie

- 550 g (1¼ lb) potatoes, boiled in their skins, peeled and mashed
- 450 g (1 lb) firm white fish fillet, such as haddock or cod
- 225 g (8 oz) smoked haddock fillet
- 1 bay leaf
- ¼ onion, sliced
- 400 ml (14 fl oz) milk
- 3 hard-boiled eggs chopped
- 65 g (2½ oz) butter
- 25 g (1 oz) plain flour
- 115 g (4 oz) peas
- 85 g (3 oz) prawns (optional)
- 2 tablespoons chopped fresh parsley
- Lemon juice to taste
- 4 tablespoons grated mature Cheddar cheese
- Salt and pepper

Poach the fish with the bay leaf and onion slices in 350 ml (12 fl oz) of the milk in a covered pan gently for 8–10 minutes. Strain and reserve the milk. Flake the fish coarsely into a pie dish, discarding the skin and any bones. Add the eggs.

Melt 25 g (1 oz) of the butter in a saucepan, stir in the flour and cook gently for 1 minute, stirring constantly. Over a low heat, gradually stir in the reserved milk. Bring to the boil, stirring, then simmer gently for about 4 minutes, stirring frequently.

Remove from the heat and add the peas, prawns (if using), parsley, lemon juice and seasoning. Pour over the fish and mix together carefully. Melt the rest of the butter gently in the remaining milk in a pan, then beat into the potato. Spoon evenly over the fish and fork up the surface. Sprinkle over the cheese and bake in a preheated 180° C (350° F/ Gas 4) oven for about 25–30 minutes.

Serves 4

Opposite above: Classic fish pie

Opposite below: Cod, prawn and mushroom gratin

Meat main dishes

In many countries, potatoes have traditionally been added to main dishes in order to make the more expensive ingredients, such as the meat, go further. This is still done today and, in addition, people who can afford meat often replace it with potatoes for health reasons.

Beef with paprika and potatoes

- 675 g (1½ lb) lean beef, cubed
- 450 g (1 lb) potatoes, peeled and cubed
- 115 g (4 oz) floury potatoes, grated
- 2 onions, chopped
- 3 tablespoons olive oil
- 1 red pepper, sliced
- 2 tablespoons paprika
- 2–3 teaspoons caraway seeds
- 1 garlic clove, crushed (optional)
- 2 tablespoons tomato purée
- 450 ml (15 fl oz) veal or vegetable stock
- 150 ml (5 fl oz) soured cream
- Salt and pepper

Brown the onions lightly in the oil in a heavy flameproof casserole. Add the beef and grated potatoes and cook for 3 minutes, then stir in the red pepper, paprika, caraway seeds and garlic (if using) for 1 minute. Add the tomato purée, stock and seasoning. Bring just to simmering point, then cover and cook gently for about 50 minutes.

Add the cubed potatoes, cover again and cook for a further 30 minutes or so, or until the beef and potatoes are tender. If the casserole becomes too dry, add more stock or water; if there is too much liquid, remove the lid toward the end of cooking.

Pour over the soured cream to give a marbled effect and heat through gently.

Serves 4

Savoury potato roulade

- 550 g (1¼ lb) potatoes, freshly mashed
- 55 g (2 oz) full-fat soft cheese with herbs and garlic or butter
- 1 egg, beaten
- 350 g (12 oz) minced) lean beef
- 115 g (4 oz) chorizo, or garlic sausage, finely chopped
- 1 small onion, chopped
- ½ red pepper, finely chopped
- 55 g (2 oz) mushrooms, chopped
- 1 tablespoon) sun-dried tomato paste or tomato purée
- Small handful fresh basil leaves, chopped
- 85 g (3 oz) Gruyère cheese, grated
- Salt and pepper

Mix the soft cheese or butter and most of the egg into the potatoes. Spread over a lightly floured 33 x 28 cm (13 x 11 in) rectangle of greaseproof paper.

Mix together the beef, sausage, onion, pepper, mushrooms and sun-dried tomato paste or purée; season. Spread over the potato and scatter with the basil leaves, pressing them in lightly.

Using the paper, roll up the potato, like a Swiss roll, starting from a short end. Carefully transfer the roll to a greased baking sheet. Brush with the remaining egg, sprinkle with the cheese and bake in a preheated oven at 180° C (350° F/Gas 4) for between 1¼–1½ hours.

Serves 4

Opposite above: Beef with paprika and potatoes

Opposite below: Savoury potato roulade

Shepherd's pie

- 900 g (2 lb) potatoes, unpeeled
- 450 g (1 lb) well-flavoured tomatoes, peeled and chopped
- 3 tablespoons olive oil
- 2 large onions, chopped
- 2 garlic cloves, crushed
- 450 g (1 lb) lean lamb, minced
- 1 tablespoon plain flour
- 25 g (1 oz) sun-dried tomatoes, chopped
- 250 ml (8 fl oz) beef stock
- 2 tablespoons chopped fresh parsley
- 3 tablespoons milk
- 55 g (2 oz) butter
- 55g (2 oz) Lancashire, feta or mature Cheddar cheese, finely crumbled or grated
- Salt and pepper

Heat the oil in a frying pan, add the onion and garlic, then sprinkle with salt and cook gently until golden and softened. Stir in the lamb until it changes colour, then stir in the flour, tomatoes, sun-dried tomatoes, stock, parsley and salt and pepper. Heat to just on simmering point, stirring constantly. Cook gently, stirring occasionally, for 30–40 minutes, or until the lamb is tender, adding a little more stock if necessary.

Meanwhile, cook the potatoes in boiling water. Drain, peel and mash with the milk, butter and seasoning.

Pour the meat mixture into a baking dish and spoon the potato on top. Sprinkle with the cheese and bake in a preheated oven at 190° C (375° F/ Gas 5) for 25–30 minutes until crisp and golden.

Serves 4

Spiced lamb and potato casserole

- 675 g (1½lb) old potatoes, cut into 4 cm (1½ in) chunks
- 1.5 kg (3 lb) lean lamb, cubed
- 2 onions, chopped
- 3 plump garlic cloves, chopped
- 1 red pepper, chopped
- 4 tablespoons chopped fresh coriander
- 1 tablespoon ground coriander
- 1 tablespoon ground cumin
- 1 teaspoon ground ginger
- 4 tablespoons olive oil, plus extra for frying
- 600 ml (1 pint) veal or vegetable stock
- 55 g (2 oz) pitted black olives
- Salt and pepper
- Fresh coriander, to garnish

Mix together the lamb, onion, garlic, red pepper, coriander, spices and oil with plenty of pepper. Cover and chill overnight.

Heat a little oil in a heavy flameproof casserole dish. Lift the meat from the marinade and brown it in the oil. Remove and reserve. Cook the marinated vegetables gently until they are soft and beginning to colour. Add the lamb, potatoes and stock, then bring just to the boil. Cover and cook in a preheated oven at 170° C (325° F/Gas 3) for about 1 hour. Add the olives and cook, uncovered, for a further 10 minutes or so. Garnish with coriander.

Serves 6

Spiced lamb and potato casserole

Baked lamb with potatoes and artichokes

- 1.1 kg (2½ lb) waxy potatoes, thickly sliced
- 1.25 kg (2¾ lb) lean lamb, cut into medium-sized pieces
- 1 onion, sliced
- Sprig fresh rosemary, broken into 3–4 pieces
- 5 tablespoons olive oil
- About 450 g (1 lb) artichokes preserved in oil, or can of artichoke hearts
- Salt and pepper

Using your hands, mix together the potatoes, lamb, onion, rosemary, oil and seasoning in a large baking tin. Bake in a preheated oven at 200° C (400° F/Gas 6) for 45 minutes. Stir the contents of the baking tin, so that the potatoes and lamb brown evenly, and cook for a further 30 minutes.

Drain the artichokes and cut them in half. Stir them into the potato mixture and bake for a further 15 minutes.

Serves 6

Baked lamb with potatoes and artichokes

Potato moussaka

- 800 g (1¾ lb) potatoes, thickly sliced
- Aubergine, weighing about 350 g (12 oz), cubed
- 2 onions, quite finely chopped
- 2 garlic cloves, crushed (optional)
- 450 g (1 lb) lean beef, minced
- ¼ teaspoon ground cinnamon
- 3 tablespoons chopped fresh parsley
- 1½ teaspoons fresh thyme
- 400 g (14 oz) can chopped tomatoes
- 1 tablespoon tomato purée
- 2 egg yolks
- 55 g (2 oz) mature Cheddar cheese, finely grated
- 350 g (12 oz) natural yogurt
- Salt and pepper

Sprinkle the aubergine with salt and leave it to drain for 1 hour. Rinse under cold running water and pat dry with paper towels.

Meanwhile, cook the potatoes in boiling salted water for 5–6 minutes. Drain thoroughly. Cook the onion, aubergine, garlic (if using), beef, cinnamon and herbs in a non-stick pan over a low heat, stirring frequently, until the meat begins to brown.

Stir in the tomatoes, tomato purée and salt and pepper, then pour the mixture into a large, shallow baking dish. Cover the top with the potato slices. Beat the egg yolks and cheese into the yogurt. Add seasoning and pour it over the potatoes. Bake in an oven preheated to 190° C (375° F/Gas 5) for 1 hour, or until the top is browned.

Serves 4

Pork, potato and fennel casserole

- 680 g (1½ lb) small new potatoes
- About 1.2 kg (2½ lb) lean pork, cut into large chunks
- 1 teaspoon chopped fresh thyme
- 1 teaspoon fennel seeds, crushed
- 2 garlic cloves, chopped
- 600 ml (1 pint) medium-bodied dry white wine
- Seasoned plain flour
- 115 g (4 oz) piece of pancetta (a type of Italian bacon), cut into thin strips
- 3 tablespoons virgin olive oil
- 2 onions, sliced
- 2 fennel bulbs
- Salt and pepper

TOPPING
- 1½ teaspoons finely grated lemon rind
- ½ garlic clove, finely chopped
- 2 tablespoons chopped fresh parsley
- Feathery fennel fronds, chopped (see method in recipe)

Mix the pork with the thyme, fennel seeds, garlic and wine in a non-metallic dish. Cover and chill for 4–12 hours, stirring occasionally.

Lift the pork from the marinade, pat dry and coat it lightly with seasoned flour. Fry the pancetta in 1 tablespoon of the oil in a heavy, flameproof casserole dish until it is lightly browned and the fat runs. Transfer to paper towels. Brown the pork in batches in the casserole. Transfer to paper towels.

Add the remaining oil and the onions to the casserole and fry gently until they are soft and beginning to brown. Stir in the marinade, bring to the boil and bubble for 2 minutes. Return the pork and pancetta to the pan. Add seasoning, cover tightly and cook gently on the hob or in a preheated oven at 160° C (325° F/Gas 3) for 1 hour.

Trim and reserve the feathery fronds of the fennel bulbs, then cut each bulb into six wedges. Add them to the casserole with the potatoes and more liquid if necessary, cover again and cook for a further 30–40 minutes, or until the pork and vegetables are tender.

Mix together the topping ingredients and scatter them over the casserole.
Serves 5–6

Dublin coddle

- 680 g (1½ lb) potatoes, sliced
- 460 g (1 lb) thick pork sausages
- 4 rashers bacon, rinded and thickly sliced
- 460 g (1 lb) onions, sliced
- Salt and freshly ground black pepper to taste

Place the sausages and bacon in a frying pan with enough water to cover; bring to the boil and simmer for 5 minutes. Drain and reserve the cooking liquid, then add the sliced onions and potatoes to the pan with plenty of seasoning.

Cover with the reserved liquid, lay a piece of greaseproof paper over the potatoes and cover the pan with a tight-fitting lid. Simmer the coddle slowly for about 1 hour, shaking the pan from time to time to prevent the contents sticking.
Serves 4

Opposite: Pork, potato and fennel casserole

Aromatic lamb with ginger and potatoes

- 900 g (2 lb) potatoes, cut into chunks
- 3 garlic cloves
- 3.75 cm (1½ in) piece of fresh ginger
- 1.2 kg (2½ lb) lean lamb, cut into 5 cm (2 in) pieces
- 4 onions, finely chopped
- 3 tablespoons oil
- 2–3 small, fresh red chillies, chopped
- Seeds from 4 cardamom pods, crushed
- 5 cm (2 in) piece of cinnamon stick
- 6 cloves
- 300 ml (10 fl oz) water
- 150 ml (5 fl oz) coconut milk
- 115 g (4 oz) cashew nuts
- Salt

Crush the garlic and ginger to make a paste, then mix it thoroughly with the meat and leave for at least 2 hours.

Heat the oil in a large saucepan and cook the onions gently until they are soft and browned. Stir in the chillies, cardamom seeds, cinnamon and cloves for 30 seconds, then add the meat. Cover and cook gently, stirring occasionally, until the moisture has evaporated.

Add the potatoes and water, bring just to the boil and cook gently until the potatoes are almost tender, adding a little more water if necessary. Add the coconut milk, cashew nuts and salt, and cook for a further 10 minutes.

Serves 4

Lamb with new potatoes and coriander

- 450 g (1 lb) lean lamb, cubed
- Seasoned flour for coating
- 350 g (12 oz) small new potatoes, halved
- 3 tablespoons olive oil
- 1 onion, chopped
- 1–2 garlic cloves, chopped
- 1 red pepper, chopped
- 1 tablespoon ground coriander
- 1 teaspoon ground ginger
- 450 ml (15 fl oz) beef, veal or vegetable stock
- 1 tablespoon Worcestershire sauce
- 1 tablespoon soy sauce
- Salt and pepper
- Chopped fresh coriander, to garnish

Toss the lamb in the seasoned flour, then brown in batches in 2 tablespoons of the oil in a heavy flameproof casserole. Using a slotted spoon, transfer to paper towels to drain.

Add the remaining oil to the casserole and cook the onion, garlic and red pepper for 2–3 minutes, then stir in the spices for 1 minute. Add the potatoes, stock, Worcestershire sauce and soy sauce. Bring to just below boiling point, then cook in an oven preheated to 180° C (350° F/Gas 4) for about 45 minutes, or until the lamb and potatoes are tender. Check the seasoning and sprinkle with chopped coriander before serving.

Serves 3–4

Opposite above: Aromatic lamb with ginger and potatoes
Opposite below: Lamb with new potatoes and coriander

Poultry main dishes

The recipes in this chapter have been selected to emphasize the versatility of potatoes, which are used in many different forms to make appetizing poultry dishes that are suitable for everyday family meals or for special occasions.

Chicken baked with potatoes and garlic

- 1.5 kg (3½ lb) chicken, cut into 12–16 pieces
- 900 g (2 lb) yellow, waxy potatoes, quartered
- 1 onion, sliced
- 20 small to medium sprigs fresh rosemary
- 20 garlic cloves, unpeeled
- 120 ml (4 fl oz) olive oil
- Salt and pepper

Mix together the chicken, potatoes, onion, rosemary, garlic and seasoning in a large, shallow baking dish. Pour over the oil and mix the ingredients again.

Bake in an oven preheated to 220° C (425° F/ Gas 7) for 20 minutes. Lower the oven temperature to 190° C (375° F/Gas 5) and cook for an additional 45 minutes, turning the chicken and potatoes occasionally, until the chicken is cooked, the potatoes are golden and the garlic is crisp.

Serves 6

Gardener's chicken

- 450 g (1 lb) small new potatoes
- 1.5 kg (3½ lb) chicken
- 3–4 thin slices lightly smoked ham, trimmed
- 12 small onions, trimmed
- 225 g (8 oz) small carrots, halved
- 225 g (8 oz) small turnips, halved
- 1 fennel bulb, quartered
- 150 ml (5 fl oz) chicken stock
- 1 bouquet garni
- Salt and pepper
- Chopped fresh parsley, to garnish

Lay the ham in a heavy flameproof casserole dish. Cover with the vegetables.

Season the chicken inside and out, then place it on top of the vegetables. Pour over the stock and add the bouquet garni. Cover tightly and cook in a preheated 200° C (400° F/Gas 6) oven for 30 minutes. Lower the temperature to 180° C (350° F/ Gas 4) and cook for a further 1¼–1½ hours. Sprinkle with the chopped parsley before serving.

Serves 4

Opposite above: Chicken baked with potatoes and garlic

Opposite below: Gardener's chicken

Chicken and leek hotpot

- 675 g (1½ lb) prepared leeks, thickly sliced
- 450g (1 lb) potatoes, unpeeled, very thinly sliced
- 1 plump garlic clove, crushed
- 3 tablespoons oil, plus extra for brushing
- 2 teaspoons plain flour
- 175 ml (6 fl oz) chicken or vegetable stock
- 120 ml (4 fl oz) medium-bodied dry white wine
- 200 g (7 oz) soft cheese with garlic and herbs
- 8 skinned and boned chicken thighs, totalling about 350 g (12 oz)
- Salt and pepper
- Fresh parsley, to garnish

Heat the oil in a flameproof casserole and cook the leeks and garlic gently until they begin to soften. Sprinkle over the flour and stir in. Pour in the stock and wine slowly, then bring to the boil, stirring all the time. Simmer for 1 minute, remove from the heat and stir in the cheese and seasoning. Add the chicken thighs, burying them in the leek mixture. Arrange the potato slices over the top, season and brush them lightly with oil.

Cover the casserole with greaseproof paper and a lid or foil. Bake in a preheated 180° C (350° F/ Gas 4) oven for 1½ hours, or until the potatoes are tender. Place the dish under a hot grill to brown the potatoes before serving garnished with the parsley.

Serves 4

Chicken, herb and lemon pie

- 550–675 g (1¼–1½ lb) freshly prepared mashed potatoes
- 4 chicken portions on the bone, each weighing about 350 g (12 oz)
- Grated rind and juice of 1 lemon
- 40 g (1½ oz) butter
- 225 g (8 oz) button mushrooms, sliced
- 2 tablespoons plain flour
- 350 ml (12 fl oz) milk
- 2 tablespoons chopped fresh chives
- 2 tablespoons chopped fresh parsley
- 1 fresh bay leaf
- 1 teaspoon fennel seeds
- 150 ml (5 fl oz) soured cream
- 4 tablespoons hot milk
- 55 g (2 oz) full-fat soft cheese or butter milk for glazing
- Salt and pepper

Toss the chicken with the lemon rind and juice and leave in a cool place for 2–4 hours, turning the chicken occasionally.

In a heavy frying pan, brown the chicken in the butter and then transfer it to a baking dish. Add the mushrooms to the butter and brown them lightly. Combine with the chicken.

Stir the flour into the pan over a low heat for 1–2 minutes. Pour in the milk slowly, stirring, and bring to the boil, still stirring, then simmer for 2–3 minutes. Remove from the heat and add the herbs, fennel seeds, soured cream, seasoning and any lemon juice left from the chicken. Pour over the chicken and mushrooms.

Whip the hot milk, seasoning and cheese or butter into the potato, then spoon over the chicken and mushrooms. Glaze with milk and bake in a preheated 180° C (350° F/Gas 4) oven for about 35 minutes.

Serves 4

Opposite above: Chicken and leek hotpot

Opposite below: Chicken, herb and lemon pie

Roast chicken with potato and fennel stuffing

- 450 g (1 lb) potatoes, cut into 1 cm (½ in) cubes
- 1.8 kg (4 lb) chicken
- 2 tablespoons olive oil
- 1 onion, finely chopped
- 55 g (2 oz) bacon, chopped
- 2 garlic cloves, crushed
- 1 fennel bulb, diced, feathery green fronds reserved
- Juice of 1 lemon
- 150 ml (5 fl oz) dry white wine
- 150 ml (5 fl oz) water
- Salt and pepper

Heat the oil in a large saucepan and fry the onion and bacon until the onion has softened but not browned. Add the garlic, potatoes and fennel, and sauté, stirring occasionally, for 10 minutes. Stir in the lemon juice and seasoning, then leave to cool.

Season the chicken inside and out and fill loosely with the potato mixture. Roast in a preheated oven at 240° C (475° F/Gas 9) for 1 hour, turning every 20 minutes. Transfer the chicken to a warm serving dish, then return to the oven with the heat turned off and the door open.

Tilt the roasting tin and spoon off the fat, leaving behind the sediment. Pour the wine and water into the pan and bring to the boil on the hob, stirring to dislodge the sediment. Serve with the chicken, garnished with the fennel fronds.

Serves 4–6

Chicken in white sauce

- 8 small new potatoes, halved if necessary
- 4 boned chicken breasts
- 55 g (2 oz) butter
- 1 small onion, chopped
- 4 small leeks, tied in a bundle
- 225 g (8 oz) celeriac, cut into chunks, or small turnips, halved
- 250 ml (8 fl oz) dry white wine (optional)
- Chicken stock or water
- 1 bouquet garni
- 150 ml (5 fl oz) crème fraîche or double cream
- Salt and pepper

Melt the butter in a large saucepan and fry the onion until it has softened but not browned. Stir in the chicken with the remaining vegetables and coat with the butter. Add the wine (if using) and enough stock or water to cover. Then add the bouquet garni and seasoning. Bring just to boiling point and cook gently for 30–35 minutes, or until the chicken and vegetables are just tender. Transfer to a warm dish and keep warm. Discard the bouquet garni.

Boil the cooking liquid vigorously until it has reduced by about two-thirds and become syrupy. Remove from the heat, stir in the crème fraîche or cream, then boil for a few more minutes to thicken it slightly. Add the chicken and vegetables, turn them in the sauce, and serve.

Serves 4

Chicken and garlic potatoes

- 900 g (2 lb) new potatoes cut into 2.5 cm (1 in) chunks
- 300 ml (10 fl oz) olive oil
- 350 g (12 oz) tomatoes, skinned and cut into chunks
- 200 g (7 oz) small onions, halved
- 3 garlic cloves, finely chopped
- 8 sprigs thyme
- 8 sprigs sage
- Salt and freshly ground black pepper
- 85 g (3 oz) pitted black olives
- 6 tablespoons peanut or vegetable oil
- 6 boneless, skinless chicken breasts
- 1¼ tablespoons finely chopped parsley

Chicken and garlic potatoes

Place potatoes in a saucepan and cover with cold, salted water; bring to the boil and simmer for 5 minutes. Drain well.

Preheat the oven to 190° C (375° F/Gas 5). Place the olive oil in a large frying pan over a medium heat. Add the potatoes, tomatoes, onions, garlic, thyme and sage. Season well and simmer for 15 minutes. Transfer to a casserole dish. Cook, covered, in the oven for 1 hour, or until the potatoes are cooked through. Add the olives during the last 15 minutes of cooking.

Meanwhile, heat the peanut oil in a large frying pan. Season the chicken fillets and fry in batches for 3–4 minutes on each side, or until browned. Slice each fillet into four. Place the chicken in a covered ovenproof dish with 115 ml (4 fl oz) water and place in the oven 15 minutes before potatoes are done.

To serve, stir the chopped parsley gently through the potato mixture and spoon on to warmed plates. Arrange the chicken slices on top.

Serves 6

Chicken with potatoes, tomatoes and fennel

- 450 g (1 lb) potatoes, boiled for 7 minutes and thinly sliced
- 4 chicken drumsticks
- 4 chicken thighs
- 55 g (2 oz) thick-cut bacon, diced
- 2 small fennel bulbs, cut into wedges, feathery fronds reserved
- 300 ml (10 fl oz) chicken stock, or 150 ml (5 fl oz) each chicken stock and dry white wine
- 225 g (8 oz) well-flavoured ripe tomatoes, quartered
- 1½ teaspoons chopped fresh thyme
- ½ garlic clove, finely chopped
- 1 teaspoon grated lemon rind
- 2 tablespoons chopped fresh parsley and reserved fennel fronds
- Salt and pepper

Dry-fry the chicken in a heavy flameproof casserole until browned and remove. Fry the bacon and fennel until it just begins to brown. Stir in the stock, and wine if using.

Return the chicken to the casserole and tuck the potatoes and tomatoes around and between the chicken pieces. Sprinkle with the thyme, garlic, lemon rind and seasoning.

Cover the casserole tightly with a lid or foil and cook in a preheated oven at 180° C (350° F/Gas 4) for 45–50 minutes, or until the chicken, potatoes and fennel are tender. Mix together the parsley and fennel fronds, and scatter over the casserole.

Serves 4

Roast goose with potato stuffing

- 1 goose, about 4.6 kg (6 lb) prepared weight
- 900 g (2 lb) cooked mashed potatoes
- 225 g (8 oz) streaky bacon, rinded and chopped
- 2 onions, finely chopped
- 1 small celery head, trimmed and chopped
- 120 g (4 oz) butter
- 225 ml (8 fl oz) milk
- 3 tablespoons freshly chopped mixed herbs
- Salt and black pepper

Preheat the oven to 160° C (325° F/Gas 3). Fry the bacon until it is crisp, then add the onions and celery and cook until they are just softened. Mix all the remaining ingredients together and add the bacon mixture, then use it to stuff the goose.

Prick the skin of the goose all over and truss the bird. Place on a trivet in a roasting tin, breast-side down, and cook for about 3½ hours. Turn the goose over halfway through the cooking time. Stand the goose for 10–15 minutes before carving, and serve with apple sauce and gravy.

Serves 6

Opposite: Chicken with potatoes, tomatoes and fennel

Side dishes

The role of potatoes as an accompanying vegetable is unsurpassed. However, too often they are just served boiled or mashed. This is a great shame because there are many ways to transform potatoes into exciting side dishes for little or no extra cost.

Baked French fries

- 675 g (1½ lb) large potatoes, unpeeled, cut length ways into 1.25 cm (½ in) slices
- 1 teaspoon chilli powder
- 1 tablespoon sunflower oil
- Salt

Put a large baking sheet in a preheated oven at 240° C (475° F/Gas 9) to heat. Place the cut potato strips in a large bowl. Toss with the chilli powder to coat them evenly, and then sprinkle them with the oil and toss again.

Arrange the potato strips in a single layer on the baking sheet and bake for about 20 minutes. Turn the strips over and bake for a further 20 minutes, or until crisp and brown. Sprinkle them with salt and serve immediately while still hot.

Serves 4

Potato and parsley galettes

- 675 g (1½ lb) waxy potatoes, peeled and coarsely grated
- 3 tablespoons chopped fresh parsley
- 2 tablespoons grated lemon rind
- 2 garlic cloves, finely chopped (optional)
- 3 eggs, lightly beaten
- 40 g (1½ oz) plain flour
- 4–5 tablespoons milk
- Salt and pepper
- Oil for frying

Mix together the potatoes, parsley, lemon rind, garlic (if using), eggs, flour, milk and seasoning to give the consistency of double cream. Heat 1 tablespoon of the oil in a frying pan. Add heaped tablespoonfuls of the potato mixture, spreading each one out to form a circle about 6 mm (¼ in) thick. Fry briskly for 2–3 minutes on each side. Using a fish slice, transfer to paper towels. Keep warm while frying the rest, adding more oil as necessary.

Makes 12–15

Opposite above: Baked French fries
Opposite below: Potato and parsley galettes

Garlic potatoes

- 450 g (1 lb) medium-sized waxy potatoes
- 4 tablespoons olive oil
- 4 garlic cloves, unpeeled
- Few sprigs of thyme or rosemary
- Crystal rock salt, to sprinkle
- Extra herbs according to taste, to garnish

Cut the potatoes lengthways into quarters and place in a bowl of cold water. Rinse under cold running water, transfer to paper towels and pat completely dry.

Heat the oil in a flameproof casserole and, when smoking hot, add the potatoes and garlic. Reduce the heat and brown the potatoes on all sides. Stir in sprigs of herbs, cover and allow to cook in their own steam for 15 minutes.

Remove the casserole lid and increase the heat to evaporate any water and crisp the potatoes. Tip the potatoes into a warm serving dish, if appropriate, and scatter with plenty of salt and more herbs, according to taste.

Serves 4

Garlic and olive oil mash

- 450 g (1 lb) floury potatoes, cut into chunks
- 1 small garlic bulb
- 55 ml (2 fl oz) milk
- 5 tablespoons extra virgin olive oil
- Salt and freshly ground black pepper
- 2 onions, finely sliced
- 1 tablespoon balsamic vinegar
- 1 tablespoon extra virgin olive oil, to serve

Preheat the oven to 200° C (400° F/Gas 6). Cut the top off the garlic bulb. Wrap the garlic loosely in foil and cook it in the oven for 20–30 minutes, or until it is soft.

Cook the potatoes in a saucepan of boiling salted water for 15–20 minutes, or until soft. Drain thoroughly and return the potatoes to the pan. Heat the milk until it is warm. Squeeze the soft garlic cloves out of their skins and add them to the potatoes. Mash the potatoes. Gradually stir in 4 tablespoons of the oil, alternating with the milk, until the potatoes reach the desired consistency. Season with salt and pepper.

Meanwhile, heat the remaining oil in a frying pan. Add the onions and cook slowly, stirring frequently, for 20 minutes, or until they are soft and golden brown. Stir in the balsamic vinegar. Top the potatoes with the fried onions, drizzle with olive oil and serve.

Serves 4

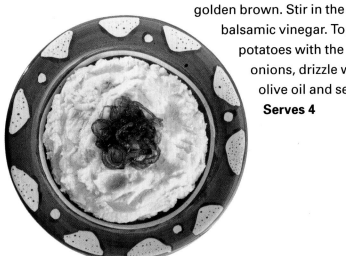

Above: Garlic potatoes

Right: Garlic and olive oil mash

Capered new potatoes

- 500 g (1 lb) new potatoes
- 3 tablespoons capers
- 90 g (3 oz) butter, softened
- Parsley sprigs, to garnish

Scrub the potatoes well and then boil them in their skins in salted water for 10 minutes. Drain and leave to cool slightly.

Meanwhile, finely chop the capers and blend them with the butter. Make a deep slit in each potato and fill with caper butter.

Tightly wrap each potato in separate squares of single-thickness foil and barbecue on a rack over hot coals for 10–15 minutes. Garnish with sprigs of parsley before serving.

Serves 4–6

Crusty garlic potatoes

- 500 g (1 lb) new potatoes
- 8–10 large garlic cloves
- 2 eggs, beaten
- 6–8 tablespoons yellow cornmeal
- Parsley sprigs, to garnish

Scrub the potatoes well and peel the garlic, leaving the cloves whole. Boil the potatoes and garlic in salted water for 12–15 minutes, or until just cooked. Drain, reserving the garlic. Skin the potatoes as soon as they are cool enough to handle. Roughly chop the garlic and, using a small skewer, insert pieces deep into the potatoes.

Dip the potatoes first in beaten egg and then in cornmeal. Press on well with a round-bladed knife, then dip in the beaten egg once more. Barbecue the potatoes on a well-oiled rack over hot coals for 10–15 minutes, or until they are crusty and golden. Serve in a basket lined with a clean napkin. Garnish with sprigs of parsley.

Serves 5–6

Above: Capered new potatoes

Right: Crusty garlic potatoes

Fried potatoes with rosemary and garlic

- 900 g (2 lb) potatoes, unpeeled, cut into 1.25 cm (½ in) cubes
- 6 tablespoons olive oil
- 6–8 plump garlic cloves, unpeeled
- Leaves from 1 sprig fresh rosemary, chopped
- Salt and pepper

Heat the oil in a large, heavy frying pan, then add the potatoes, spreading them over the base of the pan to form a single layer. Cook them over a moderate heat, stirring and turning, until they turn an even, light gold.

Scatter over the garlic cloves, cover the pan and cook for about 15 minutes, shaking the pan and stirring the potatoes occasionally, until the potatoes are tender inside and crisp and golden outside. Shortly before the end of the cooking, add the rosemary and seasoning. Serve as soon as the potatoes are ready.

Serves 4

Grilled potato slices

- 4 large potatoes, unpeeled
- 2 garlic cloves, finely chopped
- 2 sprigs fresh thyme
- 4 tablespoons olive oil
- 55 g (2 oz) butter, diced
- Salt and pepper

Boil the potatoes until they are tender. Drain, leave until they are cool enough to handle, and then peel and slice them thickly into a bowl. Add the garlic, thyme, oil and seasoning, then toss the ingredients together very gently to avoid breaking the slices. Lay the slices in an even layer on a baking sheet and place some of the diced butter on each. Cook the potatoes under a preheated grill until brown. Turn them over and cook for a further 5 minutes, or until crisp. Sprinkle them with salt and serve hot.

Serves 4

Baked potato towers

- 675 g (1½ lb) baking potatoes
- 20 g (¾ oz) butter
- 1 onion, finely chopped
- 1½ tablespoons chopped fresh chives
- Salt and pepper

Prick the potatoes all over with a fork and bake in a preheated oven at 200° C (400° F/Gas 6) for 40 minutes, or until slightly softened but not cooked through. Leave them until they are cool enough to handle and then peel and coarsely grate.

Melt the butter and cook the onion until it is soft but not brown. Mix gently with the potatoes, chives and seasoning. Spoon into eight mounds on a greased baking sheet and return to the preheated oven for another 40 minutes, or until the potato turns a golden brown.

Serves 4

Opposite left: Fried potatoes with rosemary and garlic
Opposite right: Grilled potato slices
Opposite below: Baked potato towers

Hot hot aloo

- 500 g (1 lb) small new potatoes
- 60 g (2 oz) lime pickle
- 60 ml (2 fl oz) salad oil
- 2 teaspoons tomato purée (paste)
- 2 teaspoons ground cardamom
- 2 tablespoons natural yogurt
- Lime slices, to garnish

Wash and scrub the potatoes and cook them in salt water until they are tender but still firm. Drain, leave them to cool, and then thread them on to 4–6 skewers.

Put the lime pickle in a glass bowl and, using kitchen scissors, cut up any large pieces of pickle. Blend in the oil, tomato purée (paste), cardamom and yogurt.

Spoon the pickle mixture over the skewered potatoes so that each is well coated. Barbecue on a rack over hot coals for about 10 minute, turning frequently. Garnish with the lime slices.

Serves 4–6

Potatoes Anna

- 2.5 kg (5½ lb) potatoes, finely sliced
- 125 g (4 oz) butter, melted
- Salt and pepper

Soak a clay baking dish in clean, cold water for at least 15 minutes. Brush the inside of the soaked dish with butter and then layer the potatoes, seasoning each layer well, and adding a little butter here and there. Trickle the remaining butter over the top and press the potatoes down well with the back of a spoon.

Cover the dish and place it in a cold oven. Set the oven at 220° C (425° F/Gas 7). Cook for 1½ hours. Uncover the dish and cook for a further 15 minutes. To serve, slide a palette knife between the potatoes and the dish. Invert the pot on a large platter, then lift it off to reveal the golden potato cake. Cut into wedges to serve.

Serves 8–10

Above: Hot hot aloo

Right: Potatoes Anna

Opposite left: Potatoes with pine nuts

Opposite right: Cumin potatoes with peas

Potatoes with pine nuts

- 1 kg (2 lb) small new potatoes, scrubbed
- 2 small red onions, thinly sliced
- 2 tablespoons currants
- 3 tablespoons pine nuts
- 2 tablespoons olive oil
- 2 garlic cloves, crushed
- 12 black olives, pitted and sliced
- 1 bay leaf
- Salt and pepper
- 125 ml (4 fl oz) red vermouth
- 2 tablespoons shredded basil
- Basil sprigs, to garnish

Soak a clay baking dish in clean, cold water for at least 15 minutes. Place the potatoes in the soaked dish. Mix in the onions, currants, pine nuts and olive oil. Add the garlic, olives and bay leaf with a generous sprinkling of seasoning. Pour in the vermouth. Cover the dish and place it in a cold oven. Set the oven at 230° C (450° F/Gas 8). Cook for 1 hour, or until the potatoes are tender.

Leave the potatoes to stand in the dish, without removing the lid, for 10 minutes. Then mix in the shredded basil and garnish with the whole sprigs before serving.

Serves 4–6

Cumin potatoes with peas

- 1 kg (2 lb) small new potatoes, scrubbed
- 1 large onion, chopped
- 2 tablespoons cumin seeds
- 2 tablespoons oil or melted ghee (clarified butter)
- Juice of 1 lemon
- Salt and pepper
- 250 g (8 oz) frozen peas
- 2 tablespoons chopped mint

Soak a clay baking dish in clean, cold water for at least 15 minutes. Place the scrubbed potatoes in the soaked dish and then add the onion, cumin seeds, oil or ghee and lemon juice. Sprinkle in plenty of seasoning.

Cover the dish and place it in a cold oven. Set the oven temperature at 240° C (475° F/Gas 9) and cook for 40 minutes. Next, add the peas to the dish, mixing them with the potatoes. Cook, covered, for a further 15 minutes, or until the potatoes are tender and the peas are lightly cooked. Stand for 10 minutes, without removing the lid, then mix in the mint and serve.

Serves 4–6

Potatoes with mushrooms

- 450 g (1 lb) potatoes, thinly sliced
- Olive oil for brushing
- 350 g (12 oz) brown cap mushrooms, thinly sliced
- 4 garlic cloves, crushed
- Leaves from bunch of fresh basil
- Salt and pepper

Brush with olive oil a baking dish large enough to hold the potatoes and mushrooms in a layer no more than about 4 cm (1½ in) deep. Toss the ingredients together and make an even layer in the dish. Bake in a preheated 180° C (350° F/Gas 4) oven for about 45 minutes, or until the potatoes are tender; turn over the ingredients about halfway through the cooking time. When cooked, leave for 2–3 minutes before serving.

Serves 4

New potato parcels

- 450 g (1 lb) very small new potatoes
- 55 g (2 oz) butter
- 4 sprigs fresh tarragon, thyme or rosemary
- 4 plump garlic cloves (optional)
- Sea salt

Cut four circles of greaseproof paper about 23 cm (9 in) in diameter, then cut four more slightly larger. Butter each circle.

Put one quarter of the potatoes, a herb sprig and a garlic clove (if using) on each of the larger circles. Sprinkle with salt, then cover with a smaller piece of greaseproof paper and twist the edges together to seal. Put the parcels on a baking sheet and bake in a preheated 200° C (400° F/Gas 6) oven for 20–30 minutes, depending on the size of the potatoes, until tender throughout. Serve the potatoes in their paper parcels.

Serves 4

New potato and fennel kebabs

- 450 g (1 lb) even-sized new potatoes
- 4 small fennel bulbs – if they are available, 12 baby fennel bulbs can be substituted
- Salt and pepper
- Olive oil for brushing

Halve or quarter the fennel bulbs lengthways, then cut out the central core, taking care to leave the root end intact. Meanwhile, cook the potatoes in boiling salted water for 10 minutes, then add the fennel and boil for a further 5 minutes. Drain thoroughly.

Thread the potatoes and fennel on to skewers and then brush them with olive oil, coating them on all sides. Cook under a preheated grill for 6–8 minutes, brushing frequently with oil, until they begin to char. Season before serving hot.

Serves 4

Opposite left: Potatoes with mushrooms
Opposite right: New potato parcels
Opposite below: New potato and fennel kebabs

Spicy potatoes

- 450 g (1 lb) floury potatoes, cubed
- 2 tablespoons oil
- 1 onion, chopped
- 3 garlic cloves, finely chopped
- 1 fresh red chilli, seeded and finely chopped
- 2 teaspoons cumin seeds, lightly crushed
- 55 g (2 oz) creamed coconut, quite finely chopped
- 150 ml (5 fl oz) boiling water
- 400 g (14 oz) can chopped tomatoes
- Salt
- Squeeze of lemon juice
- Sugar
- Fresh coriander or parsley, to garnish

Soak the potatoes in water for 10 minutes. Drain and dry on paper towels. Heat the oil in a large saucepan and cook the onion, garlic and chilli gently until softened but not coloured. Increase the heat, add the cumin and stir for 1 minute until its fragrance is released.

Meanwhile, stir the creamed coconut into the boiling water to dissolve. Stir the potatoes into the onion mixture to coat, then add the coconut and tomatoes. Simmer for about 25 minutes, or until the potatoes are tender. Season to taste with the salt, lemon juice and sugar. Serve garnished with coriander or parsley.

Serves 3–4

Potatoes in fresh tomato sauce

- 900 g (2 lb) potatoes, thickly sliced
- 3 tablespoons olive oil
- 2 onions, chopped
- 2–3 garlic cloves, chopped
- 550 g (1¼ lb) tomatoes, chopped
- 2 tablespoons sun-dried tomato paste or tomato purée
- 2 sprigs fresh thyme
- 1 fresh bay leaf
- 2 tablespoons chopped fresh parsley
- 300 ml (10 fl oz) vegetable stock or water

Heat the oil in a heavy casserole dish and cook the onions until softened. Add the garlic and tomatoes, and cook for 3–4 minutes, then add the sun-dried tomato paste or the tomato purée, herbs and stock or water; season. Bring to the boil, simmer for 5 minutes and then stir in the potatoes.

Cover the casserole and cook in a preheated 180° C (350° F/Gas 4) oven for about 1½ hours, or until the potatoes are tender and the sauce is thick.

Serves 4

Above: Potatoes in fresh tomato sauce

Left: Spicy potatoes

Cabbage and potato favourite

- 750 g (1½ lb) cabbage (white or green), shredded
- 4 large potatoes, thinly sliced
- 2 onions, thinly sliced
- 250 g (8 oz) rindless bacon rashers, diced (optional)
- 2 bay leaves
- Salt and pepper
- 250 ml (8 fl oz) milk
- Knob of butter

Soak a clay baking dish in clean, cold water for at least 15 minutes. Layer the cabbage, onions, potatoes and bacon (if used) in the dish, ending with a layer of potato on top. Add the bay leaves somewhere around the middle of the dish and season the layers well, especially if the bacon is not used. Pour the milk over. Cover the dish and place it in a cold oven. Set the oven at 220° C (425° F/ Gas 7), and cook for 1 hour.

Dot the potatoes with butter and cook, uncovered, for an additional 15 minutes, or until they are golden brown.

Serves 4

Colcannon

- 460 g (1 lb) cold mashed potato
- 60 g (2 oz) butter
- 120 g (4 oz) onion, leek or scallion, finely chopped
- 4 tablespoons full-cream milk
- 225 g (8 oz) cold cooked cabbage
- Salt and pepper

Melt the butter in a large frying pan. Add the onion and cook slowly until soft, then add the potato and milk with the seasonings and stir over a medium heat until the mixture is warmed through.

Beat the cooked cabbage into the potato mixture over the heat – keep stirring and beating all the time until the mixture turns pale green and becomes light and fluffy. Serve when it is thoroughly heated through.

Serves 4

Cabbage and potato favourite

Onion-flavoured potatoes

- 6 medium potatoes, peeled and finely sliced
- 1 large onion, peeled and finely sliced
- 385 ml (13 fl oz) milk
- 22 g (¾ oz) butter or margarine
- Salt and pepper

Layer the potato slices and onion in a shallow ovenproof dish and sprinkle each layer with salt and pepper.

Pour over the milk and dot with the butter or margarine. Bake, uncovered, in a preheated oven at 180° C (350° F/Gas 4) for 1–1½ hours, or until the potatoes are soft and golden brown on top.

Serves 4

Sweetcorn and potato pancakes

- About 450 g (1 lb) floury potatoes, unpeeled
- 100 g (3½ oz) cooked or canned sweetcorn kernels
- 1 tablespoon cornflour
- 1 tablespoon double cream or milk
- 1 egg, separated
- About 55 g (2 oz) butter
- Salt and pepper

Boil the potatoes until they are just tender. Drain, leave them until they are cool enough to handle, and then peel them. After peeling you need to have 300 g (10 oz) of potato. Meanwhile, spread the sweetcorn on paper towels to dry.

Pass the potatoes through a vegetable mill, potato ricer or sieve. Mix in the cornflour, cream or milk, egg yolk, sweetcorn and seasoning. Whisk the egg white until it is stiff but not dry and then fold it gently into the potato mixture.

Melt a little butter in a non-stick frying pan. Add enough of the potato mixture to form two pancakes about 1.25 cm (½ in) thick and 7.5 cm (3 in) in diameter. Cook the pancakes gently for 4 minutes on each side. Keep them hot while cooking the remaining mixture.

Serves 4

Opposite: Onion-flavoured potatoes

Cakes and breads

It will probably seem surprising to many people that cooked potatoes can be used to produce light, moist cakes and breads that keep well and taste even better. Likewise potato can be used as a topping for a tasty pizza meal.

Moist chocolate sponge cake

- 175 g (6 oz) butter
- 175 g (6 oz) caster sugar
- 115 g (4 oz) sieved cooked potatoes
- 55 g (2 oz) dark chocolate, chopped and melted
- 3 eggs, beaten
- 150 g (5 oz) self-raising flour
- 1 teaspoon baking powder
- 40 g (1½ oz) cocoa powder
- Few drops vanilla essence
- 2–3 tablespoons milk
- Whipped cream, natural yogurt or orange-flavoured light butter cream (see p. 91)
- Icing sugar, for sifting

Cream the butter and sugar together until light and fluffy. Mix in the potato and chocolate, then gradually beat in the eggs. Sift the flour, baking powder and cocoa powder over the top and fold in lightly with the vanilla essence. Add enough milk to make a soft dropping consistency.

Turn out into two buttered 20 cm (8 in) sandwich tins and bake in a preheated 180° C (350° F/Gas 4) oven for 25–30 minutes, or until set in the centre.

Leave to cool slightly, then turn out on to a wire rack to cool completely. Sandwich together with light butter cream, whipped cream or natural yogurt. Sift icing sugar over the top.

Makes a 20 cm (8 in) sandwich cake

Cider cake

- 300 g (10 oz) mixed dried fruit
- 30 g (1 oz) mixed peel
- 250–300 ml (8–10 fl oz) dry cider
- 115 g (4 oz) cooked sieved potatoes
- 115 g (4 oz) butter or margarine, diced
- 175 g (6 oz) light soft brown sugar
- 225 g (8 oz) plain flour
- 2 teaspoons mixed spice
- 1 teaspoon bicarbonate of soda
- 1 egg, beaten

Soak the dried fruit and mixed peel in the cider overnight in a covered non-metallic bowl. Transfer to a non-metallic saucepan and add the butter or margarine and sugar. Bring to the boil slowly, stirring occasionally, then simmer for 10 minutes. Remove from the heat, leave to cool slightly, then mix in the remaining ingredients to produce a soft dropping consistency.

Pour the mixture into a buttered and lined 20 cm (8 in) cake tin and bake in a preheated 180° C (350° F/Gas 4) oven for about 1¼–1½ hours, or until firm to the touch in the centre. Leave to cool for 5–10 minutes before turning out on to a wire rack. Keep for at least a day before serving.

Makes a 20 cm (8 in) cake

Opposite above: Moist chocolate sponge cake

Opposite below: Cider cake

Apple cake

- 85 g (3 oz) butter, diced
- 225 g (8 oz) self-raising flour
- Pinch salt
- ¼ teaspoon ground cinnamon
- 115 g (4 oz) light brown sugar
- 115 g (4 oz) cooked sieved potatoes
- 2 large cooking apples, peeled, cored and thinly sliced
- 2 eggs, beaten
- Milk (optional)

Rub the butter into the flour, salt and cinnamon. Stir in the sugar and potatoes, then add the sliced apples. Stir in the egg and add the milk, if necessary, to make a fairly soft consistency.

Transfer the mixture to a buttered 23 x 12 cm (9 x 5 in) loaf tin. Bake in an oven preheated to 180° C (350° F/Gas 4) for 1¼–1½ hours, or until set in the centre. Eat while warm, spread with butter.
Makes a 23 x 12 cm (9 x 5 in) cake

Light butter cream

- 55 g (2 oz) butter, preferably unsalted
- 225 g (8 oz) icing sugar
- 55 g (2 oz) cooked sieved potatoes
- Orange or lemon juice, or vanilla or almond extract to taste

Beat the butter until softened. Sift the icing sugar over the surface, then beat in until smooth and light. Beat in the potato and add flavouring to taste.
Makes 350 g (12 oz)

Fig, walnut and orange cake

- 115 g (4 oz) butter
- 225 g (8 oz) soft brown sugar
- 1 egg, beaten
- 115 g (4 oz) cooked sieved potatoes
- 350 g (12 oz) plain flour
- 1 teaspoon bicarbonate of soda
- 1 teaspoon baking powder
- 150 ml (5 fl oz) natural yogurt
- 150 g (5 oz) dried figs, chopped
- 115 g (4 oz) walnuts, chopped
- Grated rind and juice of 1 orange
- 115 g (4 oz) caster sugar

Cream the butter and brown sugar together until light and fluffy. Beat in the egg gradually, then mix in the potato until it is thoroughly combined. Sift the flour, bicarbonate of soda and baking powder over the top, then fold in lightly with a metal spoon. Stir in the yogurt, figs, walnuts and orange rind.

Turn out into a buttered 23 x 12 cm (9 x 5 in) loaf tin. Bake in a preheated 180° C (350° F/Gas 4) oven for 1¼ hours, or until a skewer inserted in the centre feels warm when withdrawn.

Mix the caster sugar and orange juice together and pour over the cake. Leave to cool for 5–10 minutes before turning out on to a wire rack to cool completely before serving.
Makes a 23 x 12 cm (9 x 5 in) cake

Opposite above: Fig, walnut and orange cake

Opposite right: Light butter cream

Opposite below: Apple cake

Potato rye bread

- 300 ml (10 fl oz) milk
- 350 g (12 oz) strong white flour
- 115 g (4 oz) freshly prepared, cooked sieved potatoes
- 115 g (4 oz) rye flour
- 1½ teaspoons easy-blend yeast
- Salt

Mash the potatoes with the milk and put into a bowl. Sift over the flours and salt, sprinkle over the yeast and mix all the ingredients together.

Knead until smooth and elastic on a lightly floured surface, then put it into an oiled bowl, cover and leave until it has doubled in volume. Knock back the dough and form it into a loaf shape. Put it into a buttered or oiled 1.5 litre (2¼ pint) loaf tin, cover and leave until it is well risen.

Bake the loaf in a preheated 220° C (425° F/Gas 7) oven for 20 minutes, then lower the oven temperature to 190° C (375° F/Gas 5) and bake for a further 20–25 minutes, or until the underneath of the loaf sounds hollow when tapped. Leave it to cool on a wire rack.

Makes a 900g (2 lb) loaf

Sun-dried tomato bread

- 450 g (1 lb) strong plain white flour
- 115 g (4 oz) freshly prepared, cooked sieved potatoes
- 2 teaspoons instant dry yeast
- 1¼ teaspoons dried oregano or mixed herbs
- 60 g (2¼ oz) sun-dried tomatoes in oil, drained and chopped
- 1 egg, beaten
- 4 tablespoons oil from the sun-dried tomatoes, or virgin olive oil
- About 250 ml (8 fl oz) mixed milk and water
- Salt and pepper

Stir together the flour, yeast, herbs and seasoning, then mix in the potatoes and sun-dried tomatoes. Make a well in the centre and add most of the egg, the oil and the mixed milk and water. Stir to a smooth dough.

Turn out on to a floured surface and knead until smooth and elastic. Put into an oiled bowl, cover and leave until it has doubled in volume.

Knock back the dough and form it into a loaf shape. Put it into a buttered or oiled 1.5 litre (2¼ pint) loaf tin, cover and leave it until well risen.

Brush with the remaining egg and bake in a preheated 220° C (425° F/Gas 7) oven for about 40 minutes, or until the base of the loaf sounds hollow when tapped. Leave it to cool on a wire rack.

Makes a 900 g (2 lb) loaf

Opposite above: Potato rye bread
Opposite below: Sun-dried tomato bread

Potato apple

- 460 g (1 lb) freshly cooked mashed potatoes
- 60 g (2 oz) butter
- 1 teaspoon ground ginger
- 4 tablespoons demerara sugar
- 60 g (2 oz) flour
- 680 g (1½ lb) cooking apples, peeled, cored and sliced
- Milk

TOPPING

- 15 g (½ oz) butter
- 1 tablespoon demerara sugar

Preheat an oven to 190° C (375° F/Gas 5). Mash the potatoes with the butter, ground ginger and 1 tablespoon of the sugar. Then add sufficient flour to make a workable dough. Divide it into two and roll out into circles of about 18 cm (7 in) diameter – one should be slightly larger than the other.

Place the larger circle on a greased baking sheet and cover it with the sliced apples and remaining demerara sugar. Dampen the edges of the potato dough, cover the apple with the remaining potato crust and seal the edges together.

Make a small hole in the top to allow the steam to escape, then glaze the crust with milk and bake for 35–40 minutes, or until the crust is browned.

When cooked, carefully widen the slit in the top of the potato apple cake and slip the extra butter and sugar in over the hot apple filling so that it caramelizes over the mixture. Serve immediately – but remember that the apple filling will be very hot.

Makes an 18 cm (7 in) cake

Potato bread

- 225 g (8 oz) potatoes
- 340 g (12 oz) strong white flour
- 120 g (4 oz) flour
- 2 teaspoons easy-blend yeast
- 1 teaspoon salt
- 30 g (1 oz) butter
- 225 ml (8 fl oz) warm water

Peel the potatoes and boil them until they are just tender. Drain and allow them to cool slightly, and then coarsely grate them.

Mix the flours with the yeast and salt; rub in the butter and add the grated potatoes. Mix to a manageable dough with the warm water, then turn out on to a floured surface and knead thoroughly, until it is smooth and fairly elastic. Shape the dough into a loaf and place it in a greased 900 g (2 lb) loaf tin. Cover with cling film or a damp tea towel and leave it to rise in a warm place for 1 hour, or until almost doubled in size.

Preheat an oven to 230° C (425° F/Gas 7). Bake the bread for 45 minutes, or until the base sounds hollow when tapped. Cool on a wire rack.

Makes a 900g (2 lb) loaf

Left: Basic potato pizza dough

Right : Potato-topped pizza squares

Basic potato pizza dough

- About 155 g (5½ oz) potato
- 345 g (12 oz) strong white flour
- 1 heaped teaspoon salt
- 3 teaspoons fresh (compressed) yeast, or 1 teaspoon dried active yeast and 1 teaspoon sugar, or 1 teaspoon easy-blend yeast
- 185 ml (6 fl oz) hand-hot water
- 1 tablespoon olive oil
- Topping, according to taste

Scrub the unpeeled potato. Boil in the skin for 30–40 minutes. Drain and allow it to cool sufficiently to remove the skin.

Put flour and salt in a large bowl. In a small bowl, cream fresh yeast with a little of the water and put in a warm place until frothy. If using dried active yeast, whisk it together with sugar and a little water and set it aside and leave until frothy. If using easy-blend yeast, mix it into the flour and salt at this stage, but do not add any liquid.

Sieve the potato directly into the flour and stir in the yeast with the remaining water. If using easy blend-yeast, add the all hand-hot water at this stage.

Mix it to a soft dough, turn it out on to a lightly floured surface and knead for 10 minutes, or until smooth. Place the dough in a clean, lightly oiled bowl and cover it with plastic wrap. Put it in a warm place for about 45 minutes, or until dough has doubled in size.

Knock back the dough and knead it briefly. Oil a 30 cm (12 in) pizza tin. Place the dough in the centre and press it out to edges with your knuckles. Pinch up the edges to create a rim. Preheat an oven to 220° C (425° F/Gas 7). Brush the dough with oil, arrange topping evenly over the top and bake for 20–25 minutes, or until it is crisp and golden.

Serves 4

Potato-topped pizza squares

- 345 g (12 oz) strong white flour
- 1 heaped teaspoon salt
- 3 teaspoons fresh (compressed) yeast, or 1 teaspoon dried active yeast and 1 teaspoon sugar, or 1 teaspoon easy-blend yeast
- 185 ml (6 fl oz) hand-hot water
- 1 tablespoon vegetable oil
TOPPING
- 8 small potatoes, peeled
- Salt
- 8 tablespoons passata
- 60 g (2 oz) Cheddar cheese, grated
- Cucumber slices and sliced spring onion, to garnish

Put the flour and salt in a large bowl. In a small bowl, cream fresh yeast with a little of the water and put in a warm place until frothy. If using dried active yeast, whisk it together with sugar and a little water and set it aside and leave until frothy. Add yeast liquid to the flour with the remaining water and oil. (To use use easy-blend yeast, mix it into the flour and salt before adding water and oil.) Mix to a soft dough and knead on a floured surface for 10 minutes. Place the dough in a clean, lightly oiled bowl and cover it with plastic wrap. Put it in a warm place for 45 minutes, or until dough has doubled.

Cook potatoes for the topping in salted boiling water for 10–15 minutes. Drain, cool slightly and thinly slice. Meanwhile, preheat the oven to 220° C (425° F/ Gas 7). Grease a Swiss roll tin. Knock back the risen dough and knead briefly. Roll out and use it to line the tin. Brush with oil.

Spread passata over dough. Arrange potato slices on top and sprinkle with grated cheese. Bake in the oven for 20 minutes. Serve cut into squares, garnished with cucumber and spring onion.

Serves 6–8

Index